CONTENTS

✦

CAMBRIDGE LITERATURE

This edition of *A Doll's House* is part of the Cambridge Literature series, and has been specially prepared for students in schools and colleges who are studying the play as part of their English course.

This study edition invites you to think about what happens when you read the play, and it suggests that you are not passively responding to words on the page which have only one agreed interpretation, but that you are actively exploring and making new sense of what you read and act out. Your 'reading' will partly stem from you as an individual, from your own experiences and point of view, and to this extent your interpretation will be distinctively your own. But your reading will also stem from the fact that you belong to a culture and a community, rooted in a particular time and place. So, your understanding may have much in common with that of others in your class or study group.

There is a parallel between the way you read this play and the way it was written. The Resource Notes at the end are devised to help you to investigate the complex nature of the writing and dramatisation process. The Resource Notes begin with the playwright's first ideas and sources of inspiration, move through to the stages of writing, publication and stage production, and end with the play's reception by the audience, reviewers, critics and students. So the general approach to study focuses on five key questions:

Who has written *A Doll's House* and why?

What type of text is it?

How was it produced?

How is it presented?

Who reads it and how do they interpret it?

The Resource Notes encourage you to take an active and imaginative approach to studying the play both in and out of the classroom. As well as providing you with information about many aspects of *A Doll's House*, they offer a wide choice of activities to work on individually, or in groups. Above all, they give you the chance to explore this epoch-making play in a variety of ways: as a reader, an actor, a researcher, a critic and a writer.

Judith Baxter

INTRODUCTION

A Doll's House opened in London in 1882 amidst controversy. *The Standard* commented, 'it would be a misfortune were such a morbid and unwholesome play to gain the favour of the public'. Its fears about the play's future were well founded. Great literary figures such as George Bernard Shaw and William Butler Yeats were very impressed with what they saw, and *A Doll's House* is now one of the most famous plays of the nineteenth century. It has been shown on television, made into film and performed in theatres all over the world.

Henrik Ibsen influenced many twentieth-century playwrights and is considered to be the founder of modern prose drama. His later plays deal with contemporary social problems; in *A Doll's House*, Ibsen explores the tragic consequences of characters accepting the false values of a society at the expense of their well-being and personal integrity.

✦ *Pre-reading activities*

The following activities can be completed individually or in pairs / small groups. They are designed to introduce you to the play and help you to record your initial reactions. You may already have your own ideas about some of the issues the play raises.

1 The play, set in Norway, was originally written in Riksmal, a written form of Danish with a Norwegian vocabulary. Ibsen said, 'anyone who wishes to understand me fully must know Norway ... the severe landscape ... and the lonely shut off life'. Think about what you already know about Norway and the images you have of it. What do you imagine life there would have been like in the nineteenth century?

2 The title of the play is *A Doll's House*. What kind of a play are you expecting it to be? Consider the following:

- What is suggested about the environment or setting of the play?
- If there is not a literal doll's house in the play, what might the title represent? What associations do the words have for you?
- Would you expect the house to belong to a male or female and what are your reasons for this?
- How important is the title of a text?

3 Errol Durbach argues that *A Doll's House* does not really capture the connotations of *Et Dukkehjem*, the original title, and that *A Doll's Home* might be more suitable (*A Doll's House: Ibsen's Myth of Transformation*, page 28). Look at the different implications of the words. After you have read the play, decide which title you think is more appropriate and why.

A Doll's House

CHARACTERS

HELMER
NORA, his wife
DOCTOR RANK
MRS LINDE
KROGSTAD
Helmer's three young CHILDREN
ANNE-MARIE, their nanny
MAID
PORTER

The action takes place in Helmer's apartment.

Act One

Room in HELMER's *apartment. The decoration is not extravagant, but comfortable and stylish. Back right, door to the hall; back left, door to* HELMER's *study. Between the doors, a piano. Centre left, a door, and beyond it a window; beside the window a round table, easy chairs and a small sofa. Upstage right, a door, and below it a stove, two easy chairs and a rocking chair. Between the door and the stove, a side-table. Engravings on the walls. A cabinet filled with china and other small objects; a small bookcase with expensively-bound books. Carpet on the floor; fire in the stove. Winter.*

A bell rings in the hall, off, and soon afterwards we hear the door being opened. Enter NORA. *She is happy, humming a tune. She is dressed in outdoor clothes, and carries a number of parcels, which she puts down on the table, right. She leaves the hall door open, and through it can be seen a* PORTER, *carrying a Christmas tree and a basket. He gives them to the* CHAMBERMAID, *who has opened the door.*

NORA Make sure you hide it, Helene. The children mustn't see it till tonight, after it's trimmed. (*To the* PORTER, *taking out her purse.*) How much is that?

PORTER Fifty øre.

NORA Keep the change. 5

The PORTER *thanks her and goes.* NORA *closes the door. She takes off her coat, laughing to herself. She takes a bag of macaroons from her pocket and eats two of them. Then she goes cautiously and listens at* HELMER's *door.*

He is home.

Still humming, she goes to the table right, and starts opening the parcels.

HELMER (*off*). Is that my little songbird piping away out there?

NORA Yes it is.

HELMER (*off*). Is that my little squirrel rustling? 10

NORA Yes.

HELMER (*off*). When did squirrelkin come home?

NORA Just now.

> *She puts the macaroons in her pocket and wipes her mouth.*

Come out here, Torvald, and see what I bought.

HELMER (*off*). Just a moment. 15

> *After a short pause, he opens the door and looks in, pen in hand.*

Did you say bought? All those? Has my little songbird been spending all my money again?

NORA Oh Torvald, this year we can let ourselves go a little. It's the first Christmas we don't have to scrimp and save. 20

HELMER That doesn't mean we've money to burn.

NORA Can't we burn just a little? A tiny little? Now you're getting such a big pay-packet, pennies and pennies and pennies.

HELMER After January the first. And even then we won't 25 see the money till the end of the first quarter.

NORA Oh fiddle, we can borrow till then.

HELMER Nora!

> *He takes her playfully by the ear.*

What a little featherbrain it is! I borrow a thousand kroner today, you spend it all by Christmas, and on 30 New Year's Eve a tile falls on my head and kills me –

NORA (*hand to mouth*). Don't say that.

HELMER But suppose it did?

NORA If it did, why would I care if I still owed people money?

35

HELMER But what about them? The people I borrowed it from?

NORA Who cares about them? I don't even know their names.

HELMER Just like a woman! But seriously, you know what I think. No borrowing. No debt. When a household relies on debt, it's slavery, it's vile. We've struggled this far without, the two of us – and we'll struggle on for a few more weeks, till we don't have to struggle any more. 45

NORA (*crossing to the stove*). Yes, Torvald.

HELMER (*following*). There, there. Poor little songbird, drooping her wings? Little squirrel, making sulky faces?
He takes out his wallet.
Nora, what have I here?

NORA (*turning quickly*). Pennies! 50

HELMER Look. (*Giving her money.*) Heavens, d'you think I don't know what it costs at Christmastime?

NORA (*counting*). Ten, twenty, thirty, forty. Oh thankyou, Torvald, thankyou. Now I'll manage.

HELMER You must. 55

NORA I will. Now come here, and see what I've bought. Bargains! A new outfit for Ivar, and a little sword. A horse and a trumpet for Bob. A dolly and a dolly's bed for Emmy. Nothing expensive: they'll soon be broken, anyway. Dress-lengths and hankies for the maids. Old 60 Anne-Marie should really have something better.

HELMER What's in this one?

NORA (*with a shriek*). No, Torvald. Not till tonight!

HELMER And what about my own little spendthrift? What would she like, herself? 65

NORA Oh fiddle. Me? I don't want anything.

HELMER Of course you do. Tell me some little thing you'd like more than all the world.

NORA I really don't … Unless … Torvald …

HELMER Yes? 70

NORA (*playing with his buttons, not looking at him*). If
you really want to give me something, you could ...
you could ...

HELMER Out with it.

NORA (*blurting it*). Give me some pennies of my own. Just 75
what you can spare. I could keep them till I really
wanted something ...

HELMER Oh, Nora –

NORA Please, Torvald, please. I'll wrap them in pretty 80
paper and hang them on the tree. They'll be so pretty.

HELMER What do they call little birds that are always
wasting money?

NORA Featherbrains. I know. But why don't we try it,
Torvald, try it? Give me time to think what I'd really
like? It would be a good idea. 85

HELMER (*smiling*). Of course it would – if you really did
manage to save it, to spend on yourself. But it'll just go
into the housekeeping, you'll spend it on this or that,
and I'll end up forking out again.

NORA No, Torvald. 90

HELMER Darling Nora, yes.

He puts his arm round her waist.

What a sweet little featherbrain it is. But it swallows
up so many pennies. It costs a lot of pennies, to keep a
little featherbrain.

NORA Don't be horrid. I do save, all I can. 95

HELMER (*with a laugh*). All you can. That's right. The
whole trouble is, you can't.

NORA (*smiling gently and playfully*). Oh Torvald,
songbirds, squirrels, you know how we spend and
spend. 100

HELMER What a funny little thing it is. Daddy's daughter.
A thousand little ways of wheedling pennies – and as
soon as you've got them, they melt in your hands. You

never know where they've gone. It's in the blood, little
Nora, it's inherited.   105

NORA I wish I'd inherited some of Daddy's other qualities.

HELMER I wouldn't have you any different. Dear little bird,
little darling. But what is it? There's something, isn't
there? There is.

NORA What?   110

HELMER Look at me.

NORA (*looking at him*). There.

HELMER (*wagging his finger*). Was little Miss Sweet-tooth
naughty in town today?

NORA What d'you mean?   115

HELMER Did she visit the sweetie-shop?

NORA No, Torvald. I promise.

HELMER She's not been nibbling?

NORA No. No.

HELMER Not one tiny macaroon?   120

NORA Torvald, I swear –

HELMER It's all right. I was only joking.

NORA (*crossing to the table right*). You told me not to.
You don't really think I'd – ?

HELMER Of course not. You promised.   125

> *He goes to her.*

Darling Nora, keep all your Christmas secrets to
yourself. They'll all come out this evening, when we
light the tree.

NORA Did you remember to invite Dr Rank?

HELMER There's no need: he'll eat with us, goes without   130
saying. I'll ask him when he comes this morning. I've
ordered good wine. Nora, you can't imagine how
much I'm looking forward to this evening.

NORA So am I. Oh Torvald, what fun the children will
have!   135

HELMER A secure job, a good income – isn't it wonderful?

NORA Wonderful.

HELMER Remember last Christmas? How you shut yourself
in here evening after evening for three whole weeks,
making tree-decorations and all the other surprises?   140
The dullest three weeks I've ever spent.

NORA I wasn't bored.

HELMER (*smiling*). It's not as if anything much came of it,
Nora.

NORA Don't be horrid. How could I guess that the cat   145
would get in and tear everything to bits?

HELMER There, there, of course you couldn't. You wanted
to please us all, that was the main thing. But thank
goodness, even so, that those hard times are past us
now.   150

NORA It's really wonderful.

HELMER No more Torvald sitting all alone and bored. No
more Nora wearing out her lovely eyes, her pretty little
fingers –

NORA (*clapping her hands*). No, Torvald, never again!   155
(*taking his arm.*) Now, shall I tell you what we ought
to do? As soon as Christmas is over –
Ring at the bell, off.
A visitor.
She begins tidying the room.
What a nuisance.

HELMER I'm not at home.   160

MAID (*at the door*). There's a lady, madam ... a stranger.

NORA Show her in.

MAID (*to* HELMER). The doctor's here too.

HELMER In the study?

MAID Yes, sir.   165

HELMER *goes into the study. The* MAID *shows in* MRS
LINDE, *who is wearing travelling clothes, and shuts the
door after her.*

MRS LINDE (*timidly, rather ill-at-ease*). Good morning,
Nora.

Nora (*hesitantly*). Good morning.

Mrs Linde You don't recognise me.

Nora No, I ... just a minute ... (*suddenly*.) Kristine!   170

Mrs Linde That's right.

Nora Kristine! To think I didn't recognise you. (*more
subdued.*) You've changed, Kristine.

Mrs Linde Nine, ten years –

Nora Is it really so long? I suppose it is. I've been so   175
happy these last eight years. And now you've come
back to town. Such a long journey, in winter too.
Aren't you brave?

Mrs Linde I came on the steamer this morning.

Nora Just in time for Christmas. What a lovely surprise!   180
What a time we'll have. Take your coat off. You can't
be cold. (*helping her.*) There. Let's be cosy, by the
stove. This armchair. I'll sit in the rocking chair.
(*taking her hands.*) That's better. Now you're like you
always were. It was just that first moment. You're   185
paler, Kristine, thinner.

Mrs Linde Older.

Nora A tiny bit.
Suddenly she breaks off, and speaks seriously.
How thoughtless of me, sitting here chattering.
Kristine, darling, I'm sorry.   190

Mrs Linde What d'you mean?

Nora (*with sympathy*). Dear Kristine, you lost your
husband.

Mrs Linde Three years ago.

Nora I read it in the paper. I did mean to write. I thought   195
about it, often. But I kept putting it off ... there was
always something ...

Mrs Linde Don't worry.

Nora It was horrid of me. Poor Kristine. Did he leave you
enough to live on?   200

Mrs Linde No.

NORA You've children?

MRS LINDE No.

NORA You've nothing?

MRS LINDE Not even sad memories. 205

NORA (*looking at her in amazement*). But surely – ?

MRS LINDE (*smiling sadly, stroking her hair*). It happens,
Nora.

NORA Completely alone. That must be awful. I've got
three beautiful children. They aren't here now, they're 210
out with Nanny. But tell me everything.

MRS LINDE No, no, you first.

NORA No, you. Today I won't be selfish. I'll put you first.
But there is just one thing – d'you know what a stroke
of luck we've had? 215

MRS LINDE What is it?

NORA They've made my husband manager. At the Bank!

MRS LINDE That's wonderful.

NORA Unbelievable. He was a lawyer. But that's not
secure, especially if you won't take on cases for people 220
you don't approve of. Torvald never would, and of
course I agree with him. But now! Imagine! He starts
in the New Year. A big salary and lots of bonuses. Our
lives'll be so different. We'll be able to do anything we
want. Oh Kristine, I'm so relieved, so happy. To have 225
no more worries, all one needs. Isn't it wonderful?

MRS LINDE Wonderful, yes, to have all one needs.

NORA Not just all one needs, but lots of money, lots.

MRS LINDE (*lightly*). Nora, Nora, have you still not grown
up? You were an extravagant little thing at school. 230

NORA (*with a light laugh*). That's just what Torvald calls
me. (*wagging a finger.*) 'Nora, Nora' – she's not all
featherbrain. Not all you both think. We've never had
the money for me to waste. We've had to work, both
of us. 235

MRS LINDE You, as well?

NORA Odds and ends. Sewing, embroidery, things like
that. (*in a low voice.*) And other things too. You know
Torvald set up on his own when we got married? He'd
no prospects at the office, and he had to earn more   240
money. In the first year, he overworked terribly. It was
because of the money. He worked every hour there
was. It was too much for him. He had a breakdown,
and the doctors said he had to get away, go South.

MRS LINDE You went to Italy, didn't you? A year in Italy.   245

NORA It was hard to get away. It was just after Ivar was
born. But we simply had to. It was wonderful,
Kristine, and it saved Torvald's life. The only thing
was, it cost a fortune.

MRS LINDE I can imagine.   250

NORA Four thousand, eight hundred kroner. A fortune.

MRS LINDE You were lucky to have it, just when you
needed it.

NORA Ah well, it came from Daddy.

MRS LINDE I remember, your father died about that time.   255

NORA Can you imagine, I couldn't go and look after him?
I was expecting Ivar, any day. Torvald was really ill.
Poor, darling Daddy. I never saw him again, Kristine.
It was the worst time of my whole married life.

MRS LINDE I know how fond you were of him. But then   260
you all went to Italy.

NORA We had the money then, and the doctors insisted.
So we went, a month later.

MRS LINDE And your husband recovered?

NORA Oh yes, yes.   265

MRS LINDE But ... the doctor?

NORA Pardon?

MRS LINDE I thought the maid said that was the doctor,
that man who arrived at the same time I did.

NORA Oh, Dr Rank. It's not because anyone's ill. An old   270
friend – he comes every day. No, since Italy, Torvald

hasn't had a moment's illness. The children are fine,
and so am I.

She jumps up and claps her hands.

Kristine, it's all so wonderful. We're so happy, so
lucky. Oh ... how awful of me. Talking of nothing but   275
myself.

She sits on a stool beside her, and rests her arms on her knee.

Don't be cross. Is it really true, you didn't love him,
your husband? Why ever did you marry him?

MRS LINDE My mother was still alive: bedridden, helpless.
I'd two younger brothers to look after. When he   280
proposed, how could I not accept?

NORA He'd money too, hadn't he?

MRS LINDE Then, he did. I think. But his business was
shaky. After he died, it collapsed entirely. There was
nothing left.   285

NORA So how did you – ?

MRS LINDE Whatever I could find. A shop ... a little school
... It's been endless hard work, these last three years. I
haven't had a moment. But now it's finished. My
mother's passed on, needs nothing more. The boys   290
have jobs, they don't need me either –

NORA You must feel so relieved!

MRS LINDE No, empty. No one left to live for.

She gets up, in distress.

I couldn't bear it any longer, life in that backwater.
Better to find something here, to occupy me, to fill my   295
mind. If I could get a job, some kind of office job –

NORA But that'll be exhausting, Kristine. Draining. You
look worn out. Why don't you go away somewhere,
have a holiday?

MRS LINDE (*crossing to the window*). Dear Nora, I've no   300
Daddy to pay the bills.

NORA (*getting up*). Don't be cross with me.

MRS LINDE (*going to her*). Nora, don't you be cross. The
    worst thing about a situation like mine is that it makes
    you hard. No one else to work for; always out for   305
    yourself; survival, it makes you selfish. You won't
    believe this: when you told me how well things were
    going for you, I was delighted – not for you, for me.

NORA Pardon? Oh. If Torvald did something for you …

MRS LINDE Yes.   310

NORA Of course he will, Kristine. Leave it to me. I'll see to
    it. I'll find a way. Put him in a good mood. I'd love to
    help you.

MRS LINDE You're so kind. To be so eager to help me.
    Especially you, when you've so little idea how difficult   315
    life can be.

NORA Me – ?

MRS LINDE (*with a smile*). Sewing, embroidering … Nora,
    you're a babe in arms.

NORA (*moving away, with a toss of the head*). Don't be so   320
    snooty.

MRS LINDE What d'you mean?

NORA You're all the same. None of you think I can
    manage anything … serious.

MRS LINDE No, no.   325

NORA You think I don't know how hard life is.

MRS LINDE But you've just told me yourself. Your
    problems.

NORA Fiddle. They were nothing. (*quietly.*) I haven't told
    you the real one.   330

MRS LINDE What real one?

NORA You don't take me seriously. You should. Aren't
    you proud of all you did, all that hard work for your
    mother?

MRS LINDE I take everyone seriously. Of course I'm proud,   335
    I made my mother's last months a little easier.

NORA And your brothers – you're proud of what you did
for them.

MRS LINDE I've a right to be.

NORA Of course you have. And so do I. I've a right to be   340
proud too.

MRS LINDE Why? What d'you mean?

NORA Sh! Torvald must never hear. He mustn't ever – no
one in the world must ever know, except you, Kristine.

MRS LINDE Know what?   345

NORA Come over here.

She pulls her to the sofa and sits beside her.

I *have* got something to be proud of. The person who
saved Torvald's life – it was me.

MRS LINDE Saved his life? How?

NORA The trip to Italy. I told you. If he hadn't gone –   350

MRS LINDE But your father –

NORA (*smiling*). That's what everyone thought. Torvald ...
everyone.

MRS LINDE But –

NORA We didn't have a penny from Daddy. I paid. I got   355
the money.

MRS LINDE All of it?

NORA Four thousand, eight hundred kroner.

MRS LINDE Nora, how? Did you win the Lottery?

NORA (*scornfully*). The Lottery! Pff! *That* wouldn't have   360
been clever.

MRS LINDE How did you get it, then?

NORA (*smiling mysteriously, humming*). Hm, hm, hm.

MRS LINDE You didn't – *borrow* it?

NORA Why not?   365

MRS LINDE A wife can't borrow without her husband's
permission.

NORA (*tossing her head*). Unless she knows about business
... knows her way around.

MRS LINDE I don't understand.   370

NORA Never mind. I didn't say I *did* borrow it. There are plenty of other ways.

She stretches out on the sofa.

Perhaps it was one of my admirers. I'm such a pretty little thing …

MRS LINDE You are silly. 375

NORA And you're nosy.

MRS LINDE Nora. Are you sure you haven't done something … rash?

NORA (*sitting up straight*). Saving my husband's life?

MRS LINDE I mean rash, if he didn't know – ? 380

NORA That's the whole point. He wasn't to know. Don't you understand? He was never to know how ill he was. The doctors came to me, to me, and told me his life depended on it. Time in the South, in the sun. D'you think I didn't try to wheedle him? I told him it 385 was for me, how lovely it would be to go abroad, like other young wives. I begged, I cried. I told him to think of my condition, he had to be kind to me, humour me. I hinted that he took out a loan. Kristine, he almost lost his temper. He said I was 390 featherbrained, and his duty as a husband was not to indulge my … my little whims, he called them. Right, right, I thought. If you won't save yourself … So I … found a way myself.

MRS LINDE Torvald never knew the money wasn't from 395 your father?

NORA Of course not. Daddy died about that time. I'd wanted to tell him, to ask him to help. But first he was too ill, then it was too late.

MRS LINDE And you've never told your husband? 400

NORA For heaven's sake! When he thinks the way he does. In any case, Torvald, a man, proud to be a man – how d'you imagine he'd feel if he knew he owed anything

to me? It would break us apart. Our lovely home, our
happiness – all gone. 405

Mrs Linde You won't ever tell him?

Nora (*thoughtfully, with a light smile*). One day. Perhaps.
When I'm not quite such a pretty little thing. Don't
laugh. I mean when Torvald isn't as smitten as he is
now, when he's tired of me dancing, reciting, dressing 410
up. Then I may need something in reserve. (*Abruptly.*)
Da, da, da. It'll never happen. Well, Kristine? What
d'you think of my great big secret? D'you still think
I'm silly? No cares in all the world? Don't think it's
been easy, meeting the payments on time, each time. 415
Quarterly accounts, instalments – I can tell you all
about that sort of thing. Keeping up with them's not
easy. I've saved a little bit here, a little bit there. Not
much from the housekeeping, because of Torvald's
position. The children couldn't go without nice 420
clothes. Every penny he gave me for my little darlings,
I spent on them.

Mrs Linde Oh, Nora! It came out of your own allowance?

Nora What else? That was mine to do as I liked with.
Every time Torvald gave me money for clothes, I put 425
half of it away. I bought the simplest, cheapest things.
Thank heavens everything looks good on me: Torvald
never noticed. But it was hard, Kristine, often. It's nice
to wear nice clothes. Don't you think?

Mrs Linde Oh ... yes, yes. 430

Nora Fortunately there were other things I could do. Last
winter I was lucky: I got a lot of copying. I locked
myself in every evening and sat and wrote, into the
small hours. It was exhausting. But it was thrilling too,
to be sitting there working, earning money. Almost 435
like a man.

Mrs Linde How much have you paid back?

NORA I really don't know. Business: it's hard to keep track
of. All I know is, I paid every penny I could scrape
together. The number of times I didn't know *how* I'd   440
manage! (*smiling.*) When that happened, I used to sit
and daydream. A rich old man was head over heels in
love with me –

MRS LINDE What? Who?

NORA Sh! He died, and when they read his will, there it   445
was in capital letters: ALL MY CASH TO BE PAID OVER
INSTANTER TO THAT DELIGHTFUL NORA HELMER.

MRS LINDE Nora! Who on Earth was it?

NORA Heavens, can't you guess? He didn't exist, he just
came into my head every time I sat here thinking how   450
to get some money. It doesn't matter now, anyway.
The silly old nuisance can stay away; I don't need him
and I don't need his will. I'm free of it! (*jumping up.*)
Free, Kristine, free of it! I can play with the children …
make the house pretty, make everything the way   455
Torvald likes it. It'll soon be spring, the wide blue sky.
We could have a holiday … the seaside. Free of it! I'm
so happy, so happy.
    A bell rings, off.

MRS LINDE (*getting up*). I'd better go.

NORA No, stay. It'll be for Torvald.   460

MAID (*in the doorway from the hall*). Excuse me, madam.
There's a gentleman here to see the master.

NORA To see the Bank Manager.

MAID Yes, madam. But I didn't know if … Dr Rank's still
there.   465

NORA Who is the gentleman?

KROGSTAD (*at the door*). Me, Mrs Helmer.
    MRS LINDE *starts, then goes over to the window.* NORA
    goes closer to KROGSTAD, *and speaks in a low, strained
    voice.*

NORA You. What is it? What d'you want with my
husband?

KROGSTAD Bank business. I work for the Bank, very junior. 470
Your husband's the new manager, and so –

NORA So it's –

KROGSTAD Business, Mrs Helmer. Nothing else.

NORA Please go in, then. Into the study.
*She inclines her head casually, closes the hall door, then
goes and starts making up the stove.*

MRS LINDE Nora, who was that? 475

NORA Krogstad. Used to be a lawyer.

MRS LINDE Oh yes.

NORA You knew him?

MRS LINDE A long time ago. He was a solicitor's clerk.

NORA That's right. 480

MRS LINDE How he's changed.

NORA Unhappy marriage.

MRS LINDE Didn't his wife die? Isn't he a widower?

NORA With a houseful of children. There, that's better.
*She shuts the stove and moves the rocking chair to one
side.*

MRS LINDE What does he do now? 485

NORA I don't know. Don't let's talk about business: it's
boring.
DR RANK comes out from HELMER's study.

RANK (*at the door*). No, no, my dear chap. I'll get out of
your way. I'll talk to Nora.
He shuts the door, then notices MRS LINDE.
Oh, excuse me. Company here as well. 490

NORA It's all right. (*introducing them.*) Dr Rank, Mrs
Linde.

RANK Dear lady. We often hear your name in this house.
Didn't I pass you on the stairs just now?

MRS LINDE I go slowly; I find stairs hard. 495

RANK You're not well?

MRS LINDE Overworked.

RANK Ah. So you came to town for our ... distractions?

MRS LINDE To find work.

RANK Is that the best cure for overwork? 500

MRS LINDE One has to live.

RANK Yes. So they say.

NORA Oh Doctor ... you know *you* want to live.

RANK Most certainly. However dreadful I feel, I want to prolong the agony as long as possible. My patients all 505
feel the same way. Not to mention those who are morally sick – one of whom, very far gone, is with Helmer even as we speak.

MRS LINDE (*distressed*). Oh.

NORA Whoever do you mean? 510

RANK Krogstad, his name is. An ex-lawyer. No one you know. Totally depraved. But even he was prattling on about how he had to *live*.

NORA Why did he want to talk to Torvald?

RANK Something about the Bank. 515

NORA I didn't know Krog – Mr Krogstad – was connected with the Bank.

RANK He's got some sort of position there. (*to* MRS LINDE.) I don't know if it's the same where you are. Some people go round sniffing out weakness ... and as 520
soon as they find it, they back the person concerned into a corner, a ... profitable corner. No escape. If you're strong, they leave you alone.

MRS LINDE You don't need curing unless you're sick.

RANK (*shrugging*). – and that makes all society a nursing 525
home.

> NORA *has been absorbed in her own thoughts; now she smothers a laugh and claps her hands.*

How else would you describe society?

NORA What do I care about silly old society? I'm laughing
at something else. Dr Rank, it's true, isn't it? Everyone
who works at the Bank has to answer to Torvald now?   530
RANK You find that funny?
NORA (*smiling, humming*). No, no. (*pacing.*) It's just odd
to think that we – that Torvald has power over so
many people. (*taking the sweet packet from her
pocket.*) Dr Rank, a macaroon?   535
RANK I thought they were forbidden.
NORA Kristine gave me these.
MRS LINDE What?
NORA It's all right. You didn't know Torvald had
forbidden them. He thinks they'll ruin my teeth.   540
Fiddle! Just once in a while. Dr Rank, don't you agree?
Have one.
> *She puts a macaroon in his mouth.*
You too, Kristine. I'll have one too. Just a little one.
Perhaps two. (*pacing again.*) I'm really so happy.
There's only one thing left –   545
RANK What's that?
NORA I'd like to say something straight out. Something to
Torvald.
RANK Why don't you, then?
NORA I daren't. It's too terrible.   550
MRS LINDE Terrible?
RANK If it's terrible, you'd better not. Say it to us, if you
like. What is it you'd say to Helmer, if he was here?
NORA I'd say – Good God!
RANK Tut, tut.   555
MRS LINDE Don't be silly, Nora.
RANK He *is* here. Say it.
NORA (*hiding the macaroon-packet*). Sh!
> HELMER *comes out of his study, with his coat over his
> arm and his hat in his hand.* NORA *runs to him.*
Torvald, darling, did you get rid of him?

HELMER Yes, he's gone.   560

NORA Let me introduce you. This is Kristine. She's come
  to town.

HELMER I'm sorry … Kristine … ?

NORA Mrs Linde, darling. Kristine Linde.

HELMER Oh yes. One of Nora's schoolfriends?   565

MRS LINDE We knew each other once.

NORA Just imagine, she's come all this way just to talk to
  you.

HELMER Pardon?

MRS LINDE No, no, I –   570

NORA Kristine's a genius at book-keeping. All she needs is
  the right man to work for, someone who'll show her
  even more than she knows already.

HELMER Very commendable, Mrs Linde.

NORA So of course, as soon as she heard that you were the   575
  new Bank Manager – they sent a telegram – she came
  here as fast as she could … Torvald, won't you find
  her something? For my sake?

HELMER It's not a bad idea. Madam, are you a widow?

MRS LINDE Yes.   580

HELMER You've book-keeping experience?

MRS LINDE A bit.

HELMER I may well have something –

NORA (*clapping her hands*). See? See?

HELMER In fact, Mrs Linde, you could hardly have come at   585
  a better time.

MRS LINDE How can I ever thank you?

HELMER Oh, that's all right. (*putting on his coat.*) But for
  the moment, if you'll excuse me …

RANK Wait. I'll go with you.   590
  He takes his fur coat and warms it at the stove.

NORA Don't be too long, darling.

HELMER An hour, no more.

NORA Are you going too, Kristine?

Mrs Linde (*putting on her coat*). I need to find a room.

Helmer We'll walk along together. 595

Nora (*helping her*). It's a shame we're so cramped here.
We just can't –

Mrs Linde No, no. Bye-bye, Nora – and thanks.

Nora Till tomorrow. Yes, come tomorrow. You too, Dr
Rank. What – if you're well enough? Of course you 600
will be. Wrap up well.

> *They go towards the hall, all talking. Children's voices on
> the stairs outside.*

They're here! They're here!

> *She runs to open the door.* ANNE-MARIE, *the nanny,
> comes in with the* CHILDREN.

Come in. Come in.

> *She bends to kiss them.* Darlings. Dear little
darlings. Kristine, aren't they darlings? 605

Rank Let's get out of the draught.

Helmer This way, Mrs Linde. This'll soon be no place to
be, except for mothers.

> *He,* RANK *and* MRS LINDE *go downstairs.* ANNE-MARIE
> *and the* CHILDREN *come into the room, followed by*
> NORA, *who closes the hall door. The* CHILDREN *chatter to
> her during what follows.*

Nora Haven't you had fun? Such rosy cheeks. Like little
red apples. Have you had a lovely time? What, both of 610
them? Emmy *and* Bob? Both on the sledge at once.
And you pulled them, Ivar? What a clever boy. Let me
hold her a moment, Anne-Marie. My own little
dolly-baby.

> *She takes the smallest* CHILD *and dances with her in her
> arms.*

Yes, Bob. I'll dance with you too. Did you? Snowballs? 615
I wish I'd been there. It's all right, Anne-Marie, I'll
take their coats off. No, no, I enjoy it. You go in. You
look frozen. There's coffee on the stove.

ANNE-MARIE *goes into the room left.* NORA *helps the*
CHILDREN *out of their coats and scatters them about, as*
the CHILDREN *all talk to her at once.*

A big dog? Ran after you? Of course it didn't bite.
Dogs don't bite dear little dolly-babies. Don't touch   620
those, Ivar. Wait and see. A surprise. Let's play a
game. Let's play ... hide and seek. Bob hide first.
What? Mummy hide first? All right. You try to find
me.

> *She and the* CHILDREN *play, laughing and shouting,*
> *running in and out of the room on the right. Eventually*
> NORA *hides under the table. The* CHILDREN *run in, but*
> *can't find her, till they hear her smothered laughter, lift*
> *up the ends of the tablecloth and see her. Shrieks of*
> *delight. She crawls out, pretending to frighten them.*
> *Louder shrieks. Meanwhile someone has knocked at the*
> *hall door, unheard. The door is half opened, and*
> KROGSTAD *appears. He waits in the doorway. The game*
> *continues.*

KROGSTAD Excuse me. Mrs Helmer.   625

> NORA *gives a stifled cry, and gets to her knees.*

NORA Ah! What is it?

KROGSTAD I'm sorry. The door was on the latch ...

NORA *(getting up).* Mr Krogstad, my husband's out.

KROGSTAD I know.

NORA Then ... what is it?   630

KROGSTAD It's you I want to talk to.

NORA Me? *(gently, to the* CHILDREN.*)* Go in there, to
Anne-Marie. What? No, the man won't hurt Mummy.
When he's gone, we'll have another game.

> *She takes the children into the room left, and shuts the*
> *door behind them. She is uneasy, and speaks tightly.*

You want to talk to me?   635

KROGSTAD Yes.

NORA It's not the first of the month.

KROGSTAD It's Christmas Eve. And what sort of Christmas
Day you have, depends on you.

NORA I can't do anything today. 640

KROGSTAD It's not that. Later. It's something else. You
have got a moment – ?

NORA Yes. Of course. I ... Yes.

KROGSTAD I was in Olsen's Restaurant and saw your
husband in the street. 645

NORA Yes?

KROGSTAD With a woman.

NORA What of it?

KROGSTAD Pardon me for asking, but was that Mrs Linde?

NORA Yes. 650

KROGSTAD Just arrived?

NORA Today.

KROGSTAD A friend of yours?

NORA I don't –

KROGSTAD Mine too. Once. 655

NORA I know.

KROGSTAD Ah. Well, I'll ask straight out: has Mrs Linde
been given a job in the Bank?

NORA Mr Krogstad, you shouldn't ask me that. An
employee. But since you have ... Yes, Mrs Linde has 660
been given a job. On my recommendation. Satisfied?

KROGSTAD I thought she had.

NORA (*pacing*). One isn't without influence. Just because
one's a woman. And employees, Mr Krogstad, people 665
in positions of dependence, should be careful not to
annoy people who, people who ...

KROGSTAD Have influence?

NORA Exactly.

KROGSTAD (*changed tone*). Mrs Helmer, you'll oblige me
by putting your influence to work for me. 670

NORA What d'you mean?

KROGSTAD You'll oblige me by making sure that I keep my
... position of dependence in the Bank.

NORA Is someone taking it away?

KROGSTAD Don't pretend you don't know. It's obvious that   675
your friend doesn't want to bump into me again – and
it's also obvious who I've got to thank for getting me
the sack.

NORA But –

KROGSTAD Never mind. I'm telling you: use your influence   680
to see it doesn't happen.

NORA Mr Krogstad, I don't have any influence.

KROGSTAD That's not what you said just now.

NORA I didn't mean ... you shouldn't have ... What makes
you think I can influence my husband?   685

KROGSTAD I've known your husband for years. He can be
influenced, Mr Manager, just like anyone else.

NORA If you're impertinent about my husband, you can
leave my house.

KROGSTAD Oh, very brave.   690

NORA I'm not afraid of you. Not any more. As soon as it's
New Year, I'll be finished with the whole business.

KROGSTAD (*with control*). Mrs Helmer, understand one
thing: if it comes to it, I'll fight for my job as if I was
fighting for my life.   695

NORA That's obvious.

KROGSTAD The money's not important. It's something else.
It's ... ah . . . You must be aware that some time ago, a
long time ago, I ... slipped up a little.

NORA I heard.   700

KROGSTAD It never came to court. But it ... blocked me,
barred doors against me. That's why I began my
business. You know what I mean. I had to make a
living – and I wasn't one of the worst. But now I want
done with it. My sons are growing up; for their sakes I   705
want to be respectable again, as much as possible.

That job at the Bank was the first step – and now your
husband is kicking me down to the mud again.

NORA Mr Krogstad, for heaven's sake, I can't help you.

KROGSTAD Can't? Won't. But I think you must.   710

NORA You'd tell my husband I owe you money?

KROGSTAD Why not?

NORA How can you? (*fighting back tears.*) My secret, my
pride, my treasure – and he hears it from *you*. It's
horrid. It'll be so *awkward*.   715

KROGSTAD *Awkward?*

NORA (*angrily*). Do it, do it, and see where it gets you. My
husband'll see what sort of man you are. You'll never
get your job back.

KROGSTAD What I meant was, is it just awkwardness   720
you're afraid of?

NORA As soon as my husband hears, he'll pay you every
penny. Naturally. At once. And then we'll be rid of
you for good.

KROGSTAD (*closer*). Mrs Helmer. Pay attention. Either   725
you've a very bad memory, or you know nothing of
business. I'd better remind you.

NORA What?

KROGSTAD Your husband was ill. You came to me for a
loan. Four thousand, eight hundred kroner.   730

NORA Where else was I to turn?

KROGSTAD I said I'd find the money –

NORA You did find it.

KROGSTAD – on certain conditions. You were so upset
about your husband, so eager for the money to cure   735
him, I don't think you noticed the conditions. So I'd
better remind you. I said I'd find the money; I wrote a
contract.

NORA And I signed it.

KROGSTAD That's right. But underneath your signature was   740
a clause saying that your father would guarantee the

repayments. Your father should have signed that
clause.

NORA He did.

KROGSTAD I left the date blank. Your father was to fill it in: 745
the date he signed the document. You remember that,
Mrs Helmer?

NORA I think so.

KROGSTAD I gave you the contract, to post to your father.
You remember that?   750

NORA Yes.

KROGSTAD You must have done it immediately, because
you brought it back in less than a week, with your
father's signature. Then I gave you the money.

NORA And I've been paying it back, haven't I? As   755
arranged?

KROGSTAD Let's keep to the point, Mrs Helmer. That must
have been a very difficult time for you.

NORA Yes.

KROGSTAD Your father was desperately ill.   760

NORA Yes.

KROGSTAD In fact he died soon after?

NORA Yes.

KROGSTAD Mrs Helmer, can you remember the exact date?
The date he died?   765

NORA 29th September.

KROGSTAD Yes indeed. I checked. That's what makes it so
extraordinary …

   He takes out a paper.

So hard to explain …

NORA What's hard to explain?   770

KROGSTAD The fact that your father signed this document
three days after he died.

NORA What d'you mean?

KROGSTAD Your father died on the 29th September. But he
dated his signature – here, look – on the 2nd October.   775
As I say, Mrs Helmer: extraordinary.

   NORA *says nothing.*

   Can *you* explain it?

   No answer.

Even more extraordinary: the words 2nd October, and
the year, aren't in your father's writing, but in
someone else's. I think I know whose. It's easily   780
explained. Your father forgot to date his signature, so
someone else dated it, someone who didn't know the
date he died. But none of that's important. What's
important is that the signature's genuine. There's no
doubt about that, is there, Mrs Helmer? This is your   785
father's signature?

   Short pause. Then NORA *lifts her head and looks defiantly
   at him.*

NORA No, it isn't. I signed father's name.

KROGSTAD Mrs Helmer, you shouldn't have admitted that.

NORA You'll get your money.

KROGSTAD Tell me: why didn't you send your father the   790
contract?

NORA He was too ill. I couldn't. I'd have had to tell him
what the money was for. He was so ill, I couldn't tell
him my husband was at death's door too. I couldn't.

KROGSTAD You should have cancelled the trip abroad.   795

NORA My husband's life! How could I?

KROGSTAD It never worried you, that you were cheating
me?

NORA I couldn't let it. I couldn't consider you. I hated you
… all that coldness, those conditions, when you knew   800
how ill my husband was.

KROGSTAD Mrs Helmer, you've obviously no idea just what
you've done. But I'll tell you, it was nothing more or
less than my own … mistake. All those years ago.

NORA You took a risk, that kind of risk, to save your wife?   805

KROGSTAD The law's not interested in reasons.

NORA Then it's a fool.

KROGSTAD Fool or not, it's what you'll be judged by, if I take this document to court.

NORA Nonsense. A daughter can't save her dying father   810
from care and worry? A wife can't help her sick husband? I know nothing about the law, but there must be laws about that. You were supposed to be a lawyer – didn't you know about them? You can't have been much of a lawyer.   815

KROGSTAD Maybe not. But contracts, the kind of contract you made with me, I know all about those. You understand? Good. Do as you please, but remember one thing: if I lose everything a second time, you keep me company.   820

He bows and goes out through the hall. NORA *is lost in thought for a moment, then tosses her head.*

NORA Ridiculous. He was trying to scare me. I'm not so silly.

She starts gathering the CHILDREN's *clothes. Stops suddenly.*

But suppose – ? No. I did it for love.

CHILDREN (*at the door, left*). Mummy, he's gone, the man.

NORA That's right, he's gone. Don't tell anyone he came.   825
Not even Daddy.

CHILDREN Mummy, let's play another game.

NORA No. No. Not now.

CHILDREN You promised.

NORA I can't just now. I'm too busy. Go in. Darlings, go   830
in.

She manages to get them out of the room and shuts the door. She sits on the sofa, takes up some sewing and does a stitch or two, then stops.

No!   835

She puts the sewing down, goes to the hall door and calls.
Helene! Bring in the Christmas tree.
She goes to the table, left, opens a drawer then stops again.
I can't. I can't.
The MAID *brings in the tree.*

MAID Where shall I put it, madam? 840

NORA There, in the middle.

MAID Can I get anything else?

NORA No thankyou. I've all I need.
The MAID *puts the tree down, and goes.* NORA *starts trimming it.*

NORA A candle here … flowers here … That dreadful
man. No, no, it's all right. The tree, the tree must be 845
beautiful. Torvald, I'll do whatever you want. I'll sing
for you, dance for you –
HELMER *comes in, with papers.*
Ah! Back so soon?

HELMER That's right. Has anyone called?

NORA No. 850

HELMER I saw Krogstad at the gate.

NORA Krogstad? Ah. He was here, just for a moment.

HELMER Nora, I know what it is. He was asking you to
put in a word for him.

NORA Yes. 855

HELMER You were to pretend it was your idea? You were
to pretend he hadn't been here? Did he ask that too?

NORA Oh, Torvald –

HELMER Nora, how could you? Talk to a man like that,
make promises, lie to me? 860

NORA Lie?

HELMER No one called, you said. (*wagging his finger.*)
Little bird must never do that again. Little bird must
only sing pretty songs. No nasties. (*putting his arm
round her waist.*) Isn't that right? Of course it is. 865

(*letting her go.*) Let's have no more about it. (*sitting by
the stove.*) It's lovely and warm in here.

> *He turns over his papers.* NORA *busies herself with the
> tree for a moment, then:*

NORA Torvald …

HELMER What?

NORA I can't wait for Boxing Day. The Stenborgs. The   870
fancy-dress party.

HELMER And I can't wait to see your surprise.

NORA I'm such a goose.

HELMER What d'you mean?

NORA The surprise. I can't think what to wear. Every idea   875
I have seems silly, silly.

HELMER Dear little Nora realises that at last?

NORA (*behind him, arms on the back of his chair*).
Torvald, are you busy?

HELMER Mm?

NORA Those papers.   880

TORVALD Bank business.

NORA Already?

HELMER The retiring manager has authorised me to review
staffing and duties. I have to do it this week, have it
ready by New Year.   885

NORA That's why poor Mr Krogstad –

HELMER Hm.

NORA (*leaning over the chair, playing with his hair at the
neck*). Torvald, if you hadn't been so busy, I was going
to ask you a big favour.

HELMER What favour?   890

NORA No one has taste like yours. I want to look nice for
the fancy-dress party. Torvald, won't you settle it? Tell
me what to wear, what I ought to go as?

HELMER Aha! My independent little creature needs a
helping hand?   895

NORA I can't manage without you.

HELMER I'll think about it. We'll sort it out.

NORA You are nice.

> *She goes to the tree. Pause.*

Aren't these red flowers pretty? Did Krogstad do
something really terrible? 900

HELMER Forged someone's name. Can you imagine?

NORA If he'd no alternative – ?

HELMER If he'd made a mistake … I'm not heartless; I
wouldn't condemn a man for one mistake.

NORA Torvald … 905

HELMER Plenty of people make mistakes, admit them, take
the punishment –

NORA Punishment?

HELMER But not Krogstad. He wriggled out of it. That's
what I can't forgive. 910

NORA You can't?

HELMER Imagine someone like that. Lies, hypocrisy,
tricking everyone in sight, his family, his wife, his
children. That's the worst thing of all, the children.

NORA What d'you mean? 915

HELMER An atmosphere like that, a stench of lies and
deceit, poisons the whole household. Each breath
children take in a house like that is a lungful of deadly
germs.

NORA (*going closer*). D'you really believe that? 920

HELMER Darling, when I worked in the law I saw hardly
anything else. Almost always, when people go bad
young in life, the cause is a deceitful mother.

NORA Just – a mother?

HELMER It's usually the mother. Though a father can be 925
just as bad. Every lawyer knows. This Krogstad has
been poisoning his children for years. Lies, cheating …
you see what I mean, depraved.

> *He holds out his hands to her.*

38

That's why darling little Nora must promise: never ask
me to help him. Mm? Mm? Take hold. What's the   930
matter? Take hold. There. I just couldn't work with
him. People like that literally make me ill.

> NORA *lets go his hands and crosses to the other side of
> the tree.*

NORA It's so hot in here. And I've such a lot to do.

HELMER (*getting up, bundling up his papers*). I must try to
get through some of this before dinner. And there's   935
your fancy dress to think about. And I may – I *may* –
have a little something in gold paper, to hang on the
tree. (*putting his hand on her head.*) My darling, my
little songbird.

> *He goes into the study and shuts the door. Pause. Then*
> NORA *whispers:*

NORA It can't be. No. It *can't*.   940

> ANNE-MARIE *appears at the door, left.*

ANNE-MARIE The children are crying for you. Shall I bring
them in?

NORA No! No! I don't want to see them. Stay with them.

ANNE-MARIE As madam wishes.

> *She closes the door.*

NORA (*white with terror*). Poison them? My children, my   945
family?

> *Pause. Then she lifts her head.*

Never. Impossible.

> *Curtain.*

Act Two

The same. In the corner beside the piano, the Christmas tree stands stripped of its decorations and with its candles burned to stumps. On the sofa, NORA's *evening cape.* NORA, *alone in the room, is pacing restlessly. She picks up her cape, then puts it down again.*

NORA Someone's coming.
> *She goes to the door and listens.*

No one. Of course not, it's Christmas Day. Not tomorrow, either. Unless –
> *She opens the door and looks out.*

No. No letters. The box is empty. (*Pacing.*) Stupid. Of course he didn't mean it. Things like that don't happen. They don't. I've got three small children.   5
> ANNE-MARIE *comes from the room left, with a large cardboard box.*

ANNE-MARIE I've found it. The box with the fancy dress.

NORA Thanks. Put it on the table.

ANNE-MARIE (*as she does so*). It needs mending.

NORA I wish I'd torn it to pieces.   10

ANNE-MARIE You can fix it. Just a little patience.

NORA I'll ask Mrs Linde to help.

ANNE-MARIE Out again? In this weather? You'll catch a chill, make yourself poorly.

NORA Never mind that … Are the children all right?   15

ANNE-MARIE Playing with their Christmas presents. If only –

NORA Are they still asking for me?

ANNE-MARIE They're used to having their Mummy there.

NORA No, Anne-Marie. I've no time any more.

ANNE-MARIE Well, little ones get used to anything.   20

41

NORA D'you think so? D'you think if their Mummy went
far away, they'd forget her?

ANNE-MARIE Far away!

NORA Anne-Marie, I want to ask you something. I've
often wondered. How could you do it? How could you   25
bear it? To give your own child to be fostered.

ANNE-MARIE I'd no choice. How else could I have been
nurse to baby Nora?

NORA But did you *want* to?

ANNE-MARIE To get such a good position? A poor girl in   30
trouble. *He* wasn't about to help.

NORA I suppose your daughter's long forgotten you.

ANNE-MARIE No, no. She wrote to me, when she was
confirmed, and when she got married.

NORA (*hugging her*). Dear old Anne-Marie. You were such   35
a good mother to me when I was little.

ANNE-MARIE Poor baby, you'd no one else.

NORA I know if my little ones had no one else, you'd …
Tsk, tsk. (*opening the box.*) Go back to them. I must
… Tomorrow you'll see how pretty I'll look.   40

ANNE-MARIE You'll be the prettiest one there.

> *She goes into the room left.* NORA *starts taking things out
> of the box, then pushes it aside.*

NORA If I dared go out. If I knew no one would come,
nothing would happen. Stupid. No one's coming.
Don't think about it. Brush my muff. What pretty
gloves. Think about something else. One, two, three,   45
four, five, six … (*screams.*) Ah! Someone's there!

> *She tries to go to the door, but can't move.* MRS LINDE
> *comes in from the hall, where she has taken off her coat.*

It's you, Kristine. There's no one else out there? Oh,
thanks for coming.

MRS LINDE They said you'd called and asked for me.

NORA I was passing. Something you can perhaps help me   50
with. Let's sit on the sofa. Look. There's a fancy-dress

party tomorrow. The Stenborgs. The apartment
upstairs. Torvald wants me to go as a Neapolitan
fishergirl, and dance the tarantella I learned in Capri.

MRS LINDE Quite a show. 55

NORA Torvald insists. This is the dress. Torvald had it
made for me. But it's all torn … I don't …

MRS LINDE It's easy. The frill's come undone, here and
here. That's all. Have you a needle and thread? Ah yes.

NORA It's kind of you. 60

MRS LINDE (*sewing*). So tomorrow you'll be all dressed up?
I'll pop in, see how you look. I never said thankyou for
that lovely evening, yesterday.

NORA (*getting up, pacing*). It could have been even better.
If you'd come to town sooner. Well. Torvald certainly 65
knows how to make a place welcoming.

MRS LINDE And so do you. Not your father's daughter for
nothing. Is Dr Rank always as gloomy as yesterday?

NORA He was bad. He's seriously ill. Lesions in the spine.
Poor man. His father was horrible. Woman after 70
woman. That's why the son … tainted blood …

MRS LINDE (*putting down the sewing*). Nora, how do you
know about things like that?

NORA (*pacing*). Oh, fiddle, if you've got three children,
people are always calling. Married women. Medical 75
things … they mention this and that … they know.

MRS LINDE (*resuming her sewing, after a short pause*).
Does he come every day, Dr Rank?

NORA He's been Torvald's best friend for years. Since they
were children. My friend too. One of the family.

MRS LINDE You're sure he's … all he seems? Not just … 80
making himself agreeable?

NORA Of course not. Why d'you think so?

MRS LINDE When you introduced us yesterday, he said he'd
often heard my name here. But your husband had no
idea who I was. So how could Dr Rank – ? 85

NORA That's no mystery. Torvald's so fond of me, wants
me all to himself, he says. He was always so jealous, if
I mentioned people I'd known before. So I didn't. But I
often gossip with Dr Rank. He enjoys all that.

MRS LINDE Nora, you are a child, sometimes. Listen to me. 90
I'm older, more experienced. Finish all this with Dr
Rank.

NORA Finish all what?

MRS LINDE Yesterday you talked about a rich admirer,
someone who'd leave you all his money – 95

NORA That's right. Imaginary, alas. What of it?

MRS LINDE Is Dr Rank ... well off?

NORA Oh yes.

MRS LINDE No dependants?

NORA What about it? 100

MRS LINDE Calls here every day?

NORA I told you.

MRS LINDE How could a good friend be so ...
presumptuous?

NORA I don't know what you mean. 105

MRS LINDE Nora. Don't pretend. D'you think I can't guess
who lent you all that money?

NORA You're crazy. A friend, who calls in every day –
d'you think I could bear it?

MRS LINDE It isn't him? 110

NORA Of course it isn't him. I'd never have dreamed ... In
any case, in those days he hadn't a penny to lend. He
came into money later.

MRS LINDE That could be lucky for you.

NORA Dr Rank? You don't think I'd ever ask him ... ? 115
Though I'm sure if I did ...

MRS LINDE Which you won't.

NORA Of course I won't. But if I *did* ...

MRS LINDE Behind your husband's back?

NORA I'll finish with the other one. That's also behind his   120
back. I've got to finish it.

MRS LINDE I said so yesterday. But –

NORA (*pacing*). It's easy for a man to end that kind of
thing. But a wife …

MRS LINDE Her husband could do it.   125

NORA Oh no. (*stands still.*) When you pay off a debt, you
do get your contract back?

MRS LINDE I imagine so.

NORA And you can tear it to bits, burn the nasty, filthy   130
thing.

> MRS LINDE *looks at her, then puts down the sewing and*
> *goes to her.*

MRS LINDE What is it, Nora?

NORA What?

MRS LINDE Something's happened since yesterday.

NORA (*going close*). Kristine … (*listens.*) Sh! Torvald.
Look, go in there, with the children, d'you mind?   135
Torvald hates seeing dress-making. Anne-Marie'll help
you.

> MRS LINDE *gathers some of her things.*

MRS LINDE All right, but I won't leave the house till we've
talked about this properly.

> *She goes into the room, left, as* HELMER *comes in from*
> *the hall.*

NORA (*going to greet him*). Darling. I've been waiting …   140

HELMER Was that the dressmaker?

NORA No, Kristine. She's helping me. I'll look splendid.

HELMER Wasn't it a good idea?

NORA And aren't I good to do it?

HELMER (*chucking her under the chin*). Good, to agree   145
with your husband? Tut, tut, tut. Well, I'll keep out of
the way. You'll be wanting to try it on.

NORA You've work to do?

HELMER Yes. (*showing her a sheaf of papers.*) I've just
 been into the Bank …   150
 He is about to go into the study, when she stops him.
NORA Torvald.
HELMER Yes?
NORA If your little squirrel asked for something, very, very
 nicely …
HELMER Yes … ?   155
NORA Would you do it?
HELMER Depends what it was.
NORA If you'd be good and kind and say yes, little squirrel
 would dance and do lots of tricks.
HELMER Come on.   160
NORA Little songbird would chirp and sing in every room.
HELMER Songbird does that anyway.
NORA I'd play fairies, dance in the moonlight. Torvald.
HELMER Nora: this isn't what you were asking this
 morning?   165
NORA (*going to him*). Eth, Torvald. I'th athking vewwy
 nithely.
HELMER How can you bring that up again?
NORA Please. For me. Give Krogstad his job back. Please.
HELMER Nora, darling, I've given Mrs Linde Krogstad's   170
 job.
NORA And that was very kind of you. But surely you can
 sack some other clerk instead of Krogstad.
HELMER I don't believe this. Obstinacy! Because *you* made
 him a stupid promise, *I'm* supposed to –   175
NORA Torvald, that isn't why. It's for your sake. He writes
 articles in dreadful newspapers. You told me so. He
 can do you a lot of harm. I'm scared of him, scared –
HELMER Because of the past.
NORA What d'you mean?   180
HELMER Well, obviously: your father.

NORA Oh. Yes. When those spiteful men wrote about him in the papers. Lies and slander. He'd have lost his job if you hadn't been sent to enquire, if you hadn't been so kind to him, so helpful … 185

HELMER Nora, there's a vital difference between your father and me. Your father wasn't a respected public official. I am. And I hope I'll always be so, as long as I stay in office.

NORA Who knows what terrible things they'll do, those 190 men? We could be so happy here, Torvald, you, me, the children, in our carefree, peaceful home. All I ask, please –

HELMER It's because you plead for him that I can't help him. Everyone at the Bank knows I've sacked him. If it 195 comes out that the new manager changes his mind when his wife demands it –

NORA What's wrong with that?

HELMER You mean if my little terrier got her way? I'd be a laughing stock. Before the whole staff. They'd think 200 anyone could work on me. I couldn't have that. In any case, I can't take Krogstad back, under any circumstances.

NORA Why not?

HELMER I could overlook his character if I had to – 205

NORA Of course you could.

HELMER And they say he's a good worker. But I knew him when we were both children. We were friends – one of those stupid friendships you regret later in life. I mean, we used first names. And that tactless oaf won't let it 210 lie, even now, even when we're in company. Thinks it's quite in order to stroll up any time he feels like it – 'Hey, Torvald, Torvald … ' Highly embarrassing. It would make my position in the Bank impossible.

NORA Torvald, you're joking. 215

HELMER You think so?

NORA I can't believe you're so small-minded.

HELMER You think I'm small-minded?

NORA Of course I don't. So –

HELMER Right. You think I'm small-minded.   220
Small-minded. I'll settle this right away.
He goes to the hall door and calls:
Helene!

NORA What are you doing?

HELMER (*fishing among his papers*). Settling it.
The MAID *comes in.*
Here. Take this letter. Run downstairs, find a porter   225
and tell him to deliver it. Right now. The address is on
it. Here's some money.

MAID Yes, sir.
She goes. HELMER *gathers his papers.*

HELMER Now then, little Miss Stubborn …

NORA (*hardly able to breathe*). Torvald, what was it, that   230
letter?

HELMER Krogstad's dismissal.

NORA Call her back, Torvald. There's still time. Oh
Torvald, call her back – for me, for you, for the
children. Please, Torvald, please. You don't know   235
what it'll do to us.

HELMER Too late.

NORA Yes, too late.

HELMER Darling, I don't blame you for being upset, even
though it's so insulting to me. That's right, insulting.   240
To think that I'd be afraid of that … that worn-out
pen-pusher. I don't blame you, because it shows how
much you love me. (*taking her in his arms.*) My own
dear darling, this is how it'll be. Whatever happens, I'll
be strong enough, brave enough. I'm a man, I'll carry   245
the burden alone.

NORA (*terrified*). You mean – ?

HELMER All of it.

NORA (*recovering her composure*). You'll never have to do
    that.   250

HELMER Darling, we'll share it, then: husband and wife.
    That's how it'll be. (*stroking her.*) Happy? It's all right,
    all right. Poor little trembling dove. Silly, silly. Why
    don't you play that tarantella? Practise your
    tambourine. I'll go into the office and shut the door. I   255
    won't hear; make all the noise you want.
        He goes to the door, then turns.
    When Rank comes, tell him where to find me.
        *He nods to her, goes into the study with his papers and
        shuts the door.*
        NORA *stands rooted, terrified and unsure.*

NORA (*whisper*). He was ready to do it. He can. He will.
    Nothing can stop him. No. He mustn't. But how?
    What?   260
        Doorbell, off.
    Rank! Anything …
        *She passes her hands over her face, pulls herself together
        and goes to open the door to the hall.* RANK *is in the hall,
        hanging up his coat. During the scene which follows, it
        begins to get dark.*
    Hello, Doctor. I recognised your ring. Don't disturb
    Torvald: he's busy just now.

RANK What about you?
        He comes into the room, and she shuts the door.

NORA You know I've always got time for you.   265

RANK Thankyou. I'll make the most of it, as long as I can.

NORA As long as you can?

RANK What's the matter?

NORA It sounded odd, that's all. As if you were expecting
    something to happen.   270

RANK I've been expecting it for a long time. Not quite so
    soon, that's all.

NORA (*taking his arm*). What is it? Doctor, tell me.

RANK (*sitting by the stove*). I'm done for. Incurable.

NORA (*sighing with relief*). Oh, it's you.   275

RANK No point lying to oneself. Mrs Helmer, I'm in the worst state of all my patients. I've spent the last few days reviewing my own case. Terminal. In a month I'll be rotting in the churchyard.

NORA Don't be horrid.   280

RANK It is horrid. And it won't get any less horrid. One more examination; as soon as that's done, I'll know the exact moment when the decline begins. Mrs Helmer, one thing. Torvald's a fastidious man. Ugliness disgusts him. I won't have him in my   285
sickroom.

NORA Doctor –

RANK Absolutely not. Door barred. As soon as I know the worst, I'll send you one of my cards, marked with a cross. You'll know that the dissolution, the vileness,   290
has begun.

NORA You're being ridiculous. I wanted you to be in such a good mood …

RANK With Death at my elbow? For someone else's guilt? How fair is that? I think it's the same in every family   295
in the world: retribution, one kind or another, unavoidable –

NORA (*covering her ears*). La, la, la! Be nice, be nice.

RANK It's a joke. The whole thing's a joke. My father indulged himself; my poor blameless spine has to pay 300
the bill.

NORA (*at the table, left*). Foie gras? Asparagus?

RANK And truffles.

NORA Oysters.

RANK Naturally.   305

NORA Port, champagne – what a shame such delicious things take it out on our poor old bones.

RANK Especially poor old bones that never had the
pleasure of them.

NORA That's the worst of all.   310

RANK (*looking hard at her*). H'm.

NORA (*after a short pause*). Why did you smile?

RANK You were laughing.

NORA Doctor, you smiled.

RANK (*getting up*). You're even wilder than I thought.   315

NORA I'm in a wild mood today.

RANK So it seems.

NORA (*both hands on his shoulders*). Doctor, darling,
please don't die. For Torvald, for me, don't die.

RANK You'll get over me. Out of sight, out of mind.   320

NORA (*distressed*). Don't say that.

RANK You'll find someone else. People do.

NORA Who does? Who will?

RANK You. Torvald. You've started already. Mrs Linde –
why else was she here yesterday?   325

NORA Hoho. You're jealous.

RANK Of course I am. She'll take my place. When I'm
dead and done for, she'll be the one –

NORA Sh! She's in there.

RANK You see?   330

NORA She's doing some sewing. What a bear you are!
(*sitting on the sofa.*) Be good now, Doctor, and
tomorrow you'll see how nicely I dance. You can
pretend it's all for you – well, for Torvald too.
    She starts taking things out of the box.
Doctor Rank, sit down here. I want to show you   335
something.

RANK (*sitting*). What?

NORA These.

RANK Silk stockings.

NORA Aren't they pretty? It's dark now, but tomorrow ...   340
No no, look at the feet. Oh well, the legs as well.

51

RANK Hm –

NORA What's the matter? Don't you think they'll fit?

RANK I've no possible way of telling.

NORA (*glancing at him*). Tut tut!   345
    She flicks his ear with the stockings.
    Bad boy!

RANK What other delights am I to see?

NORA None at all, you're far too naughty.
    Humming, she turns the things over. Short pause.

RANK When I sit here with you, so friendly, I can't ... it's
    hard to ... what would my life have been like if I'd   350
    never known this house?

NORA (*smiling*). You really feel at home here.

RANK (*low, looking straight ahead*). To have to leave it
    forever –

NORA Fiddlededee. You don't.   355

RANK (*as before*). To have to leave without a single token
    of what it's meant to me ... hardly a backward glance
    ... just an empty place for the next person, anyone, to
    fill ...

NORA What if I asked you ... No!   360

RANK Asked what?

NORA For a token. Of friendship ...

RANK Go on.

NORA I mean, a really big favour.

RANK I'd be delighted –   365

NORA You don't know what it is, yet.

RANK Tell me.

NORA I can't. It's too much. Advice, help, a favour –

RANK The bigger the better. I can't imagine what you
    mean. Tell me. Don't you trust me?   370

NORA You're my truest, dearest friend. You know you
    are. Doctor, it's something you can help me prevent.
    You know how Torvald loves me ... deeply, beyond
    words ... he'd give his life ...

RANK (*leaning forward to her*). Nora. D'you think he's the   375
   only one?

NORA (*starting*). What?

RANK The only one who'd give his life for you?

NORA (*heavily*). Ah.

RANK I swore I'd tell you before I ... went. Now. Nora,   380
   now you know. And you know that you can rely on
   me, as on no one else.

NORA (*getting up, calmly and evenly*). Excuse me.

RANK (*sitting still, but making room for her to pass*).
   Nora –

NORA (*at the hall door*). Helene, bring the lamps.   385
   She crosses to the stove.
   Doctor, dear Doctor, that was uncalled for.

RANK (*getting up*). To love you as much as ... another
   man? Uncalled for?

NORA To tell me. There was no need.

RANK You knew?   390
   The MAID *brings in the lamps, puts them on the*
   table and goes out again.
   Nora ... Mrs Helmer ... are you saying you knew?

NORA I don't know what I knew. How could you be so ...
   clumsy?

RANK All that matters is, you know I'm at your service,
   body and soul. Tell me what it is.   395

NORA (*staring at him*). What?

RANK Please.

NORA Not now.

RANK Don't punish me. Let me help you ... whatever a
   man can do.   400

NORA There's nothing you can do. I don't really need
   help. It was just ... a game, a silly game.
   She sits on the rocking chair, and smiles at him.
   Doctor, what a man you are! Aren't you embarrassed,
   now, in proper light?

RANK Not in the least. But perhaps I'd better go ... forever. 405
NORA Of course not. Come. Don't change. You know
what it means to Torvald.
RANK And to you?
NORA I'm always delighted to see you.
RANK That's why I ... I don't understand you. I've often 410
thought that you enjoy my company almost as much
as Torvald's.
NORA Company. We enjoy some people's company.
Others, we love.
RANK Yes. 415
NORA When I was a child, I loved Daddy more than
anyone. But I kept thinking how nice it would be to
slip down to the servants' room. They never told me
what to do. They were such fun to talk to.
RANK And it's *their* place I've taken. 420
    NORA *jumps up and goes to him.*
NORA I didn't mean that. I didn't mean that. It's just that
... Torvald and Daddy ... Don't you see?
    The MAID *comes in.*
MAID Madam ...
    She whispers to her and gives her a visiting card.
NORA (*glancing at it*). Ah!
    She puts it in her pocket.
RANK Nothing wrong? 425
NORA No, no. Just ... my new dress.
RANK It's in there, your dress.
NORA One of them is. This is another one. I ordered it ... I
don't want Torvald to know.
RANK Hoho. *That* was the great big secret. 430
NORA Yes. Go in to him now. He's in the study. Keep him
there.
RANK Don't worry. He won't get away.
    He goes into the study.
NORA (*to the* MAID). He's in the kitchen? Waiting?

MAID He came to the back door. 435

NORA You told him no one was in?

MAID It didn't do any good.

NORA He wouldn't go?

MAID He said he had to talk to you.

NORA Well, bring him in. But quietly. Helene, keep it a 440
secret. It's a surprise for my husband.

MAID Yes, madam. I understand.

She goes.

NORA It's happening. I can't stop it. I can't. I can't.

She locks the study door. The MAID *ushers* KROGSTAD
*in from the hall, and shuts the door behind him. He is
wearing boots and a fur coat and cap.* NORA *hurries
to him.*

NORA Keep your voice down. My husband's here.

KROGSTAD Doesn't matter. 445

NORA What d'you want?

KROGSTAD I want you to explain something.

NORA Be quick.

KROGSTAD You know I've been sacked?

NORA There was nothing I could do. I tried, but it was no 450
good.

KROGSTAD Your husband cares so little for you? He knows
the harm I can do you, and still he –

NORA What makes you think he knows?

KROGSTAD Ah. I thought he didn't. I could hardly imagine 455
Torvald Helmer being so brave –

NORA I'll thank you to show a little more respect.

KROGSTAD As much as he deserves. But since milady's kept
the whole thing so carefully to herself, I imagine it's
sunk in since yesterday, exactly what you've done. 460

NORA No thanks to you.

KROGSTAD I'm a very bad lawyer, remember?

NORA What is it you want?

KROGSTAD Mrs Helmer, I was anxious about you. I've had
you in my thoughts all day. A cashier, a pen-pusher, a   465
nonentity like me, can still feel sympathy.

NORA Feel some, then. For my children.

KROGSTAD As much as you and your husband felt for me?
Never mind. I just want to tell you, there's no need to
take this business to heart. There'll be no accusations   470
made from this side.

NORA I didn't think there would be.

KROGSTAD It can be settled easily. Amicably. No one has to
know but the three of us.

NORA My husband must never find out.   475

KROGSTAD How will you prevent that? Are you saying you
can pay the balance?

NORA Not at the moment.

KROGSTAD You've some quick way to find it?

NORA None I intend to use.   480

KROGSTAD In any case, it wouldn't help now. However
much you pay, I'm not giving up that paper.

NORA What are you going to do with it?

KROGSTAD Keep it, that's all. Safe. No third party need ever   485
hear of it. So if you'd any crazy ideas –

NORA I had.

KROGSTAD – of running away, for example –

NORA Who told you?

KROGSTAD – don't bother.

NORA How did you know I – ?   490

KROGSTAD We all think of that at first. I did, too. But I
wasn't brave enough.

NORA (*tonelessly*). Neither am I.

KROGSTAD (*lightly*). Exactly. You aren't brave enough,
either.   495

NORA No.

KROGSTAD It would be stupid, anyway. Once the first
storm at home blows over ... I've a letter here for your
husband.

NORA Telling him everything?   500

KROGSTAD As objectively as possible.

NORA (*blurted*). He mustn't see it. Tear it up. I'll find the
money.

KROGSTAD I'm sorry, Mrs Helmer, but I thought I just told
you –   505

NORA I don't mean the loan. Tell me how much you're
demanding from my husband, and I'll find the money.

KROGSTAD I'm not asking him for money.

NORA What, then?

KROGSTAD I told you. Mrs Helmer, I want to make myself   510
respectable. I want to get on. I want your husband to
help me. I've had clean hands for eighteen months, and
things have been very difficult. I didn't mind: I was
working my way up, step by step. But now I've been
sacked, I won't be satisfied with simply getting my job   515
back. I want something better. Reinstatement – in a
higher position. Your husband will find one –

NORA He won't.

KROGSTAD I know him. He won't dare argue. Once I'm
back, just wait and see! In one year – less – I'll be the   520
Manager's right hand. Not Torvald Helmer, but Nils
Krogstad, will run that bank.

NORA No. Never.

KROGSTAD You mean you'll – ?

NORA I'm brave enough now.   525

KROGSTAD You don't scare me. A fine lady, airs and graces
–

NORA Wait and see.

KROGSTAD Under the ice, perhaps? In the deep, dark
depths? Floating up in the spring, bloated,   530
unrecognisable, your hair fallen out –

NORA You don't scare me.

KROGSTAD And you don't scare me. Mrs Helmer, no one does things like that. In any case, what good would it do? I'd still have him just where I wanted him.   535

NORA You mean even after I ... even if I was – ?

KROGSTAD Have you forgotten? I own your reputation.

    NORA *stares at him speechlessly.*

So, you stand warned. Don't do anything stupid. Helmer will get my letter. I'll wait for a reply. And remember this: it was him, your husband, who forced   540
me to do this. I'll never forgive him for that. Good afternoon.

    He goes out through the hall. NORA, *at the door, holds it open and listens.*

NORA He's going. He's not leaving the letter. Of course he is. (*opening the door further.*) What is it? He's standing there. Not going downstairs. He's changing   545
his mind. He's –

    A letter falls into the box, and we hear KROGSTAD's *steps dying away as he goes down the stairs. With a stifled shriek,* NORA *crosses to the table by the sofa. Short pause.*

In the letter-box.

    She creeps across to the hall door.

Torvald, oh Torvald, he's finished us.

    MRS LINDE *comes in from the room left. She carries the fancy dress.*

MRS LINDE That didn't take long. Shall we try it on – ?

NORA (*hoarse whisper*). Kristine, come here.   550

MRS LINDE (*throwing the costume down on the sofa*).

What's the matter? You look terrified.

NORA Come here. D'you see that letter?

MRS LINDE Yes.

NORA It's from Krogstad.

MRS LINDE The man who lent you the money?   555

NORA Now Torvald'll know everything.

MRS LINDE It's really best, for both of you.

NORA You don't understand. I forged a signature.

MRS LINDE For heaven's sake!

NORA Kristine, you must speak for me. 560

MRS LINDE What d'you mean?

NORA If I ... go crazy.

MRS LINDE Nora.

NORA Or if anything happened ... if I had to go away ...

MRS LINDE What are you saying, Nora? 565

NORA If someone else wants to take all the blame – d'you understand? –

MRS LINDE Yes.

NORA *Then* you must speak for me. I'm not crazy. I know what I'm doing. And I'm telling you: no one else knew 570 anything about it. I did it, not another soul. Remember.

MRS LINDE I still don't understand.

NORA Why should you understand? What's going to happen ... is a miracle!

MRS LINDE A miracle? 575

NORA It's a miracle. And it mustn't happen, Kristine, mustn't happen for all the world.

MRS LINDE I'm going to see Krogstad.

NORA No. He'll hurt you.

MRS LINDE Once, he'd have done anything for my sake. 580

NORA Krogstad?

MRS LINDE Where does he live?

NORA I don't ... (*fishing in her pocket.*) Yes, here's his card. But the letter, the letter ...

HELMER (*in his room, knocking*). Nora! 585

NORA (*scream*). Ah! What is it?

HELMER Don't be alarmed. We won't come in. You've locked the door. Are you trying the dress?

NORA Yes. Yes. I'll be so pretty, Torvald.

MRS LINDE (*who has read the card*). It's just round the 590 corner.

Nora It's too late. We're finished. The letter's in the box. There, in the hall.

Mrs Linde And your husband has the key?

Nora The only one.   595

Mrs Linde Krogstad must ask for his letter back, unopened. He must find some excuse …

Nora But it's now that Torvald always –

Mrs Linde Delay him. Go in there. I'll be as quick as I can.

She hurries out through the hall. NORA *goes to* HELMER's *door, opens it and peeps in.*

Helmer (*out of sight*). Ah! We can use our own front   600
room again. Come on, Rank, now we'll see – (*in the
doorway.*) What's the matter?

Nora What d'you mean, darling?

Helmer Rank said I was to expect a transformation.

Rank (*in the doorway*). I must have been mistaken.   605

Nora No one's to admire my dress till tomorrow morning.

Helmer Nora, you look worn out. Have you been
practising too hard?

Nora I haven't been practising.

Helmer You ought to.   610

Nora I will, Torvald. But you've got to help. I can't
remember it all.

Helmer We'll soon bring it back.

Nora Yes, Torvald, help me. Promise. I'm terrified … all
those people. Help me, this evening. No business. No   615
pen, no papers. Please, Torvald.

Helmer I promise. This evening I'm yours, and yours
alone. Little Miss Helpless. Just a moment, though –
He makes for the hall door.

Nora Where are you going?

Helmer Just to see if the post has come.   620

Nora Torvald, don't.

Helmer What's the matter?

Nora Torvald, I beg you. There isn't any.

HELMER I'll just have a look.

> *He is about to go, when* NORA *runs to the piano and plays the first few bars of the tarantella. He stops.*
Aha!   625

NORA I can't dance tomorrow, unless I rehearse with you.

HELMER (*going to her*). You're really nervous?

NORA Let me practise. There's time, before dinner. Please,   630
Torvald, sit down and play for me. Play, and watch,
and put me right.

HELMER Of course. Whatever you like.

> *He sits at the piano.* NORA *takes a tambourine and a long shawl out of the box. She drapes herself in the shawl, jumps centre front and cries:*

NORA I'm ready! Play!

> HELMER *plays and she dances.* RANK *looks on, standing by the piano.*

HELMER Slower, slower.

NORA This way.

HELMER Not so violently.   635

NORA Yes. Yes.

> HELMER *stops playing.*

HELMER It isn't right.

NORA (*laughing, swinging the tambourine*). I *told* you.

RANK Let me play.

HELMER (*getting up*). Good idea. I'll be able to see better.   640

> RANK *sits and plays.* NORA *dances, ever more wildly.*
> HELMER *has taken his place by the stove, and directs her as she dances. She seems not to hear him. Her hair falls over her shoulders, and she pays no attention. She is engrossed in the dance.* MRS LINDE *comes in, and stands at the door, amazed.*

MRS LINDE Ah!

NORA (*as she dances*). Look, Kristine, look!

HELMER Nora, darling, anyone'd think your life depended
on this dance.

NORA It does.   645
HELMER Rank, stop. This is ridiculous. Stop.
    RANK *stops playing, and* NORA *stands suddenly still.*
    HELMER *goes to her.*
  It's incredible. You've forgotten the whole thing.
NORA (*throwing down the tambourine*). I *told* you.
HELMER You need a lot of practice.
NORA Yes, Torvald. I must practise, and you must watch.   650
  Like you did before. Please, Torvald, please.
HELMER I said I would.
NORA Today, tomorrow, concentrate on me. Nothing else.
  No letters. Don't even open the postbox.
HELMER You're still afraid of him.   655
NORA Yes.
HELMER He's written a letter. It's here.
NORA I don't know. I think so. But don't read it. Not
  now. Nothing nasty must come between us, not now,
  not now.   660
RANK (*aside to* HELMER). Better humour her.
HELMER (*taking her in his arms*). Whatever my darling
  wants. But tomorrow night, when you've done your
  dancing –
NORA Then you're free.   665
MAID (*at the door, right*). Madam, dinner's served.
NORA We'll have champagne, Helene.
MAID Yes, madam.
    She goes.
HELMER What do I hear? A celebration?
NORA A banquet, all night long. Champagne! (*calling.*)   670
  And macaroons, Helene. Platefuls of macaroons!
    HELMER *takes her hands.*
HELMER Calm down. Sh, sh. Little singing bird, there there.
NORA Go in. You too, Doctor. Kristine, help me put up
  my hair.
RANK (*to* HELMER *as they go in*). She's not … ah … ?   675

HELMER No, no, no. My dear fellow! Over-excited, that's all.

> *They go out, right.*

NORA Well?

MRS LINDE Gone. Out of town.

NORA I knew. As soon as I saw you. 680

MRS LINDE He'll be back tomorrow afternoon. I wrote him a note.

NORA I wish you hadn't. You can't stop it. A miracle's going to happen, and we're celebrating.

MRS LINDE What miracle? 685

NORA You can't guess. Go in. I won't be long.

> MRS LINDE *goes into the dining room.* NORA *stands quite still, as if gathering herself. Then she looks at her watch.*

Five o'clock. Seven hours till midnight. Then twenty-four hours till tomorrow midnight. Twenty-four and seven. Thirty-one. Thirty-one hours left, to live. 690

> HELMER *comes to the door, right.*

HELMER What's keeping my little singing bird?

NORA Here she is! Here!

> *She runs to him with open arms.*
> *Curtain.*

Act Three

The same. The table and chairs have been moved centre. There is a lighted lamp on the table. The hall door is open, and dance-music can be heard from the upstairs apartment. MRS LINDE *is sitting at the table, turning the pages of a book. She is trying to read, but finds it hard to concentrate. She looks at her watch.*

MRS LINDE Still not. It's almost time. Perhaps he won't –
    She listens again.
Here he is.
    She goes into the hall and carefully opens the main door. Light steps can be heard on the stairs outside. She whispers:
Come in. There's no one here.

KROGSTAD (*in the doorway*). You left me a note. What is it?

MRS LINDE I must talk to you.　　　　　　　　　　　　　　　5

KROGSTAD Here?

MRS LINDE Not at my lodgings: I don't have my own entrance. Come in. There's no one here. The servants are asleep, and the Helmers are upstairs at a party.

KROGSTAD (*coming in*). A party? Tonight of all nights?　　10

MRS LINDE Why shouldn't they?

KROGSTAD No reason.

MRS LINDE Nils, we've got to talk.

KROGSTAD Do we?

MRS LINDE It's important.　　　　　　　　　　　　　　15

KROGSTAD Really?

MRS LINDE You've never understood.

KROGSTAD What's to understand? It was obvious to anyone. A heartless woman, jilting a man as soon as a better chance turned up.　　　　　　　　　　　　　20

MRS LINDE Heartless? D'you really think so? You think it was easy?

KROGSTAD Wasn't it?

MRS LINDE You really thought so?

KROGSTAD If it wasn't, why did you write ... what you wrote? 25

MRS LINDE What else could I do? I had to break with you. It was essential to kill everything you felt for me.

KROGSTAD (*wringing his hands*). Yes. I see. And all that ... for money. 30

MRS LINDE I'd a bedridden mother and two small brothers. We couldn't wait for you, Nils. You'd no prospects then.

KROGSTAD You'd no right to throw me away for someone else. 35

MRS LINDE Who can judge?

KROGSTAD (*slowly*). When I lost you, it was like being shipwrecked. Look: I'm drowning.

MRS LINDE Help may be near.

KROGSTAD It was near, until you came and interfered. 40

MRS LINDE Until today, I'd no idea it was your job they were giving me.

KROGSTAD If you say so. But now you know. What will you do now – turn it down?

MRS LINDE That wouldn't help you. 45

KROGSTAD What's help to do with it?

MRS LINDE Life, hard need ... I've learned.

KROGSTAD And I've learned to distrust fancy speeches.

MRS LINDE Fine words, yes. But deeds?

KROGSTAD What d'you mean? 50

MRS LINDE You said you were drowning.

KROGSTAD It's true.

MRS LINDE Well, so am I. No one to weep for, to care for.

KROGSTAD You chose it.

MRS LINDE I had to – then. 55

KROGSTAD What d'you mean?

MRS LINDE Nils, two drowning people – can't we help each other?

KROGSTAD You –

MRS LINDE Two together, support each other. 60

KROGSTAD Kristine.

MRS LINDE Why else d'you think I came?

KROGSTAD You thought of me?

MRS LINDE All my life, as long as I can remember, I've worked. It's been my greatest pleasure, my only 65
pleasure. Now I'm alone … empty, thrown away.
Where's the satisfaction in working for oneself? Nils,
give me someone, something to work for.

KROGSTAD Hysteria. Female hysteria. Extravagant
self-sacrifice, that's what this is. 70

MRS LINDE From *me*?

KROGSTAD You know … all about me? My past?

MRS LINDE Yes.

KROGSTAD And what I count for here?

MRS LINDE You said just now, hinted, that if I'd been with 75
you things would have been different.

KROGSTAD Quite different.

MRS LINDE And now?

KROGSTAD Kristine, you mean this. I can see it. You really
would – 80

MRS LINDE I need someone to mother; your children need a
mother; you and I need each other. I trust you, Nils,
the man you really are.

KROGSTAD (*taking her hands*). Thankyou. Kristine,
thankyou. Now I can … climb again. No. I forgot … 85

MRS LINDE Sh! The tarantella. Go, now.

KROGSTAD What?

MRS LINDE As soon as it's done, they'll be coming.

KROGSTAD I'll go. But there's nothing we can do. You don't
know what … steps I've taken with the Helmers. 90

MRS LINDE Nils, I do.

KROGSTAD And still you – ?

MRS LINDE Despair – I know what it makes people do.

KROGSTAD If I could only cancel it.

MRS LINDE You can. Your letter's still there, in the box at   95
the door.

KROGSTAD (*giving her a long look*). It's her you want to
save. Your friend. That's what this is.

MRS LINDE Nils, someone who's sold herself once for
someone else, doesn't do it twice.   100

KROGSTAD I'll ask for my letter back.

MRS LINDE No.

KROGSTAD Yes. I'll wait for Helmer. I'll tell him I want my
letter … it's just about my dismissal … he's not to read
it …   105

MRS LINDE No, Nils. You mustn't. Don't ask for it back.

KROGSTAD That's why you wrote, why you asked me here.

MRS LINDE It was, yesterday. I was in a panic. But since
then, you won't believe the sights I've seen in this
house. Helmer must know the truth. The secret must   110
come out. No more lies, tricks, they must understand
each other.

KROGSTAD Whatever you say. But there's one thing I can
do, and I'll do it now.

MRS LINDE (*listening*). Hurry. Go. They've finished. We're   115
not safe a moment longer.

KROGSTAD I'll wait downstairs.

MRS LINDE Yes: they may see me to the door.

KROGSTAD This is the luckiest day of my life!

He goes out through the hall, leaving the hall door open.
MRS LINDE *tidies the room, and puts her coat ready to
put on.*

MRS LINDE At last. Someone to work for, live for. A home.   120
There. It's all I want. If only they'd *come*.
She listens.

They're here. Coat on.

    HELMER *and* NORA *can be heard off: Key in the door,*
    then HELMER *all but pulls* NORA *into the hall. She is*
    wearing the Italian dress and a large black shawl; he is in
    evening dress, with a black, swirling cloak. NORA *stands*
    in the doorway, resisting.

NORA No. No. I want to go back up. It's too soon, too
soon.

HELMER Nora, darling – 125

NORA Please, Torvald. Please. Another hour. For little
Nora. Please.

HELMER No, darling. Not another minute. We agreed.
Go in. You'll catch cold out here.

    She still resists, but he brings her into the room.

MRS LINDE Good evening. 130

NORA Kristine!

HELMER Mrs Linde, good evening. Isn't it rather late – ?

MRS LINDE I'm sorry. I was dying to see Nora in her dress.

NORA You've been sitting, waiting?

MRS LINDE I just missed you, you'd gone upstairs. I 135
couldn't go home again without seeing you.

HELMER (*taking off* NORA's *shawl*). Well, here she is. Isn't
she pretty? Isn't she delightful?

MRS LINDE She's –

HELMER They all thought so, upstairs. But what an 140
obstinate little thing it is. What are we to do with her?
D'you know, I almost had to steal her away by force.

NORA Torvald, it would have been all right. Just half an
hour.

HELMER You see, Mrs Linde? She danced her tarantella. 145
A triumph. As well it should have been. A little …
energetic, a little more … enthusiastic than artistic …
but still a triumph. Was I going to let her stay after
that? Spoil the effect? Of course I wasn't. I took my
little Capri fishergirl – my delicious, capricious little 150

fishergirl – on my arm … swift tour round the room, curtsy here, curtsy there – and the vision of loveliness was gone, as they say in fairy tales. Always make a good exit, Mrs Linde – that's what I keep telling her. Fff, it's hot in here. 155

He throws his cloak over a chair, and opens the study door.

Dark? It's dark. Excuse me.

He goes into the study and lights a couple of candles. Meanwhile, NORA *whispers to* MRS LINDE, *quickly and breathlessly:*

NORA Well?

MRS LINDE (*in a low voice*). I've talked to him.

NORA And – ?

MRS LINDE Nora, you must tell Torvald. Everything. 160

NORA (*tonelessly*). I knew it.

MRS LINDE You've nothing to fear from Krogstad. But you must tell Torvald.

NORA I won't do it.

MRS LINDE Then the letter will. 165

NORA Thanks, Kristine. Now the miracle – Sh!

HELMER (*coming back in*). Well, Mrs Linde? Have you gazed your fill?

MRS LINDE I'll say goodnight.

HELMER Is this yours, this knitting? 170

MRS LINDE (*taking it*). I'd forgotten all about it.

HELMER You knit as well?

MRS LINDE Yes.

HELMER Have you ever tried embroidery?

MRS LINDE Why? 175

HELMER Far more becoming. Look, when you embroider, you hold the frame like this, in the left hand, the needle like this, in the right hand … a graceful, easy movement …

MRS LINDE Yes. 180

HELMER Whereas knitting ... no gracefulness ... elbows in, needles pumping up and down ... chopsticks ... That was wonderful champagne.

MRS LINDE Good night, Nora. And no more obstinate.

HELMER Well said! 185

MRS LINDE Good night, sir.

HELMER (*going to the door with her*). Good night, good night. You'll find your way home? I could easily ... no, it's just round the corner. Good night, good night.

She goes, and he shuts the door and comes back into the room.

What a boring woman! 190

NORA Torvald, you must be tired.

HELMER Not at all.

NORA Sleepy?

HELMER Wide awake, full of beans. What about you? You look exhausted. 195

NORA I must go to bed.

HELMER You see! I was right, to make you come away.

NORA You're always right.

HELMER (*kissing her forehead*). That's it. Little singing 200 bird, making lots of sense. Did you notice Rank this evening? How happy he was?

NORA I hardly spoke to him.

HELMER Neither did I. But I've seldom seen him so jolly.

He looks at her for a moment, then goes closer.

H'm. It's so nice to be back home again, just the two of us. Just you, and me. 205

NORA Torvald.

HELMER My darling. No one else's. My sweetheart, my treasure.

NORA *goes to the other side of the table.*

NORA Don't look at me like that.

HELMER (*following her*). Aha! Little Miss Tarantella still? 210 More delicious than ever. Listen! The guests are leaving. (*in a low voice.*) Nora, soon it'll be so still, so still ...

NORA I hope so.

HELMER Darling, you know when I'm out with you, at a   215
party, when I hardly talk to you, just glance at you
now and then – d'you know why I do that? I'm
pretending we're secret lovers, that we're promised to
one another, and it's our secret, no one knows but us.

NORA I know you were thinking of me.   220

HELMER When it's time to come away, and I'm arranging
the shawl on your pretty shoulders, your lovely neck, I
imagine you're my new young bride, we've just come
from the wedding, I'm bringing you home for the very
first time ... we're alone for the very first time ...   225
alone, my shy little, sweet little darling. All evening
I've longed for nothing else but you. When I saw you
twirling, swirling in the tarantella, my blood pounded,
I couldn't bear it, I hurried you, hurried you down
here –   230

NORA Torvald! Let me go! I won't!

HELMER Darling, you're joking, it's a game. Won't?
Won't? I'm your husband.

   Knock at the outer door.

NORA (*startled*). Listen!

HELMER (*at the hall door*). Who is it?   235

RANK (*off*). Me. Can I come in a moment?

HELMER (*low, crossly*). What does he want? (*aloud.*) Just a
minute.

   He goes and opens the door.

   Nice of you to drop by.

RANK I thought I heard you. Just wanted to make sure.   240

   He glances all round.

   Yes, yes. These dear, familiar rooms. Such a happy,
cosy little home.

HELMER I see you enjoyed the party too.

RANK Of course. Why shouldn't I? Why shouldn't we
enjoy every blessed thing? As much as we can, as long   245
as we can. Good wine –

HELMER Especially champagne.

RANK I was amazed how much I managed to put away.

NORA Torvald drank plenty too.

RANK Really?   250

NORA It goes straight to his head, always.

RANK No harm in a ... jolly evening after a well-spent day.

HELMER Well-spent? I can't quite claim that.

RANK (*slapping his back*). But I can, I can.

NORA Scientific work, Doctor Rank? Investigation?   255

RANK Exactly.

HELMER Such big words for such a little girl! Scientific ...
investigation ...

NORA May I congratulate you on the result?

RANK Indeed you may.   260

NORA A good one?

RANK For the doctor, and the patient, the very best.

NORA (*eagerly, anxiously*). Final?

RANK Final. So didn't I deserve a jolly evening, after that?

NORA Oh doctor, of course you did.   265

HELMER Hear, hear. So long as you don't regret it in the
morning.

RANK No one must ever regret anything, ever.

NORA You really enjoy fancy-dress parties?

RANK If there are plenty of pretty costumes.   270

NORA So what will we go as next time, you and I?

HELMER Little featherbrain, thinking of next time already.

RANK You and I? I know: you can be a good-luck pixie.

HELMER What on Earth will she wear for that?

RANK Just her ordinary clothes.   275

HELMER Bravo! How gallant! And what will you go as?

RANK I know, exactly.

HELMER What?

RANK At the next fancy-dress party, I shall be – invisible.

HELMER Brilliant! 280

RANK There's a big black hat – haven't you heard of it?
You put it on … invisible.

HELMER (*checking a smile*). Absolutely right.

RANK But I'm forgetting what I came for. Helmer, give me
a cigar, one of the dark Havanas. 285

HELMER Delighted.

He offers him the case. RANK *takes a cigar and cuts the
end.*

NORA (*striking a match*). Let me light it for you.

RANK Thankyou.

He holds out the cigar, and she lights it.
And now, goodbye.

HELMER Goodbye, dear old friend, goodbye. 290

NORA Sleep well, Doctor.

RANK Thankyou.

NORA Say the same to me.

RANK If you like. Sleep well. And thanks for the light.
He nods to them both, and goes out.

HELMER (*glumly*). Too much to drink. 295

NORA (*absently*). Perhaps.

HELMER *takes keys out of his pocket and goes into the
hall.*
Torvald! What are you doing?

HELMER The letter-box is full. If I don't clear it, they'll
never get the papers in tomorrow.

NORA You're not going to work tonight. 300

HELMER You know I'm not. Hello. Someone's been at the
lock.

NORA The lock?

HELMER Yes. But who? Not the servants … A broken
hairpin. Yours, Nora. 305

NORA (*quickly*). One of the children must have –

HELMER Make sure they never do it again. Hm, hm ...
there. Done it.

He takes the letters out and shouts to the kitchen.

Helene! Helene! Put out the front door lamp.

He comes in and shuts the hall door. He has the letters in his hand.

Just look at them all.   310

He turns them over.

What's this?

NORA (*at the window*). No, Torvald!

HELMER Two visiting cards – from Rank.

NORA Rank?

HELMER (*looking at the cards*). Lars Johan Rank, Bachelor   315
of Medicine. They were on top. He must have posted
them when he went out just now.

NORA Is there anything on them?

HELMER A cross of some kind, over the name. Look. What
an odd idea. You'd think he was announcing his own   320
death.

NORA He was.

HELMER You know about this? He told you?

NORA He said, when the card came, it was to say   325
goodbye. He'll lock himself in, to die.

HELMER My friend. My poor friend. I knew we wouldn't
have him long. But so soon, and shutting himself away
like a wounded animal.

NORA If it has to happen, it's better without a word. Don't
you think so?   330

HELMER (*pacing*). He was like family. I can't imagine him
... gone. Unhappy, lonely – he was like the sky, and
our happiness was the Sun. Well, perhaps it's best. For
him, anyway. (*standing still.*) And perhaps for us too,
Nora. We've no one else now, just each other.   335

He puts his arms round her.

Darling wife, I can never hold you tight enough. D'you
know, I've often wished you were in some deadly
danger, so that I could give my heart's blood, my life,
for you.

NORA (*firmly, disengaging herself*). You must open those   340
letters, Torvald.

HELMER Not tonight. I want to be with you, darling. With
my wife.

NORA But Rank, think of Rank –

HELMER Yes. It's come between us – ugliness, death, a   345
reminder of death. We must try to shake it off. Till
then – separate rooms.

    NORA *throws her arms round him.*

NORA Darling, sleep well, sleep well.

HELMER (*kissing her forehead*). Sleep well, little songbird.
Sleep well, Nora. I'll read those letters now.   350

    He takes the letters into the study and shuts the door.
    NORA, *wild-eyed, fumbles round, takes his cloak and*
    throws it round herself. She speaks in a hoarse, broken
    whisper.

NORA Never again. Never see him again. Never.

    She puts her shawl over her head.

The children ... never again. Never. Water ... deep ...
black ... Soon, soon, if only ... He's opened it. He's
reading it. Nothing, now. Torvald, little ones, goodbye

–   355

    She is about to hurry out through the hall, when HELMER
    opens the study door and stands there. He holds an open
    letter.

HELMER Nora.

NORA (*scream*). Ah!

HELMER You know what this letter says?

NORA I know. Let me go. Let me out.

HELMER Where are you going?   360

    He holds her back. She struggles.

NORA You won't save me, Torvald.

HELMER (*stumbling*). It's true? What he writes, it's true? Unbearable. It's not, it can't be –

NORA It's true. You were more than all the world to me.

HELMER Never ... mind ... that. 365

NORA (*going to him*). Torvald!

HELMER How could you?

NORA Let me go. Don't help me. Don't take it over. Please.

HELMER Stop playing games.

He locks the hall door.

You're staying. You have to come to terms. D'you 370
understand what you've done? Do you understand?

NORA (*looking straight at him; frost forming in her voice*). Now, I understand.

HELMER (*pacing*). To wake up to this! Eight years ... my joy, my life, my wife ... Lies, deceit ... a criminal. No way out. No end. 375

He stops and looks at her. She returns his gaze, without a word.

I should have expected it. I should have known. Like father – sh! – like daughter. No religion, no ethics, no sense of duty. I shut my eyes to what he was like – for your sake, for you – and this is what I get. This is how you repay me. 380

NORA This is how I repay you.

HELMER You've killed my happiness. You've destroyed my future. I'm trapped, in his claws. No mercy. He'll do whatever he likes to me, demand, insist, I can't refuse. No way out. A silly, empty-headed woman – and now 385
I'm dead.

NORA When I'm out of your way, you'll be free of it.

HELMER Don't ... talk. Your father was just the same. Talk! Even if you're out of the way, as you put it, what good is that to me? He'll tell his tale. They'll think I 390
knew what you were doing, that I was part of it.

Behind it, even – that the whole thing was my idea.
And this from you, the wife I supported and cherished
throughout our marriage. Now d'you understand what
you've done to me? 395

NORA (*icy*). Entirely.

HELMER It's beyond belief. I can't believe it. But it's
happened; we have to cope with it. Take off that
shawl. Take it off! I must try and calm him. It *must* be
hushed up. Whatever it costs. As for you and me, we 400
must go on as if nothing had changed between us. In
public. You'll stay on here, obviously. But I won't have
you near the children. I can never trust you again.
Fancy having to say that to you – the woman I loved, I
still … no. It's gone. Happiness is gone. Rags, crumbs, 405
pretence …

Doorbell, off. He jumps.

At this hour? It can't be, not *him*. Nora, hide yourself.
Say you're ill.

She stands motionless. He unlocks the hall door.
The MAID *is in the hall, in her nightclothes.*

MAID A letter. For madam.

HELMER Give it me. 410

He takes the letter and shuts the door.

Yes. It's from him. Leave it. I'll read it.

NORA You read it.

HELMER (*by the lamp*). I … can't. It could be the end of us,
both of us. No, I must.

He tears open the letter, reads a few lines, then shouts
with joy:

Nora! 415

NORA *looks at him enquiringly.*

Nora … no, just let me check. Yes, yes. I'm saved.
Nora, I'm saved.

NORA And me?

HELMER You as well. Naturally. Both of us are saved. He's
sent your contract back. Writes that he's sorry ... his   420
life has changed ... what does it matter what he
writes? We're saved. No one can touch you. Nora,
Nora – wait. First these must be got rid of. H'm ...
He glances at the contract.
No, I won't look at it. Forget it, a nightmare.
He tears the document and the letters in pieces, stuffs
them in the stove and watches while they burn.
There you are: finished. He said that ever since   425
Christmas Eve you've – Nora, these last three days
have been dreadful for you.

NORA I've fought hard these last three days.

HELMER Racking yourself, no way out – no, don't let's
think about it. It was dreadful; it's over; let's shout for   430
joy. Nora, don't you understand? It's over. What's the
matter? Such an icy face. Oh darling, Nora, I know
what it is. You can't believe I've forgiven you. I have, I
promise. Forgiven you everything. I know that
everything you did, you did because you loved me.   435

NORA Yes.

HELMER You loved me as all wives should love their
husbands. You were new to it, that's all: you didn't
understand what you were doing. But don't think I
love you any less, just because you don't know how to   440
manage things. I'll guide you, darling, I'll protect you.
Lean on me. I'd hardly be a man, if feminine weakness,
your weakness, didn't make me love you even more.
Those hard words, when I thought everything was lost
– forget them. I've forgiven you, Nora, I swear I've   445
forgiven you.

NORA You're very kind.
She goes out, right.

HELMER Wait. (*looking in.*) What are you doing?

NORA (*off*). Changing. No more fancy dress.

HELMER (*at the open door*). Yes. Good. Be calm, be calm,   450
my frightened little bird. Nothing will hurt you; I'll
spread my wings, I'll shelter you. (*pacing by the door.*)
It's warm and cosy, our nest, our home. Nothing will
hurt you. Poor frightened dove, I'll save you from the
hawk, I'll keep you safe. Still, little fluttering heart, be   455
still. It'll be all right. Darling, you'll see. Tomorrow ...
it'll all be like it was before. You'll soon understand, I
won't need to remind you I've forgiven you. I'll never
abandon you, never blame you – how can you think
so? A husband's love, darling – a true husband's heart,   460
how can you understand it? How sweet, how
satisfying, to feel that he's forgiven his wife, from the
depths of his being, forgiven her? Made her twice his
own: given her life, identity, his wife, his child. That's
what you are to me now, poor, helpless little darling.   465
Don't ever be frightened, Nora. Tell me the truth, and
your will, your conscience – leave both to me. But
what – ? Not going to bed? You've changed.

NORA (*in her ordinary clothes*). I've changed.

HELMER But why now? It's late.   470

NORA I won't sleep tonight.

HELMER Nora, darling –

NORA (*looking at her watch*). It's not very late. Sit here,
Torvald. We have to come to terms.

    She sits at one side of the table.

HELMER Nora? So cold –   475

NORA Sit down. There's a lot to say.

    HELMER *sits facing her across the table.*

HELMER Nora? I don't understand.

NORA Exactly. You don't understand me. And I've never
understood you – until just now. Don't say anything.
Listen. It's time to come to terms.   480

HELMER What d'you mean?

NORA (*after a short pause*). It's strange. Isn't it?

HELMER What is?

NORA We've been married eight years. And this is the first
time we've sat down together, you and me, husband   485
and wife, to talk seriously.

HELMER Seriously.

NORA In eight years – no, since the first day we met –
we've never talked seriously about a single thing.

HELMER You didn't expect me to tell you my worries all   490
the time – things you couldn't help me with?

NORA I don't mean business. I mean, we've never sat
down and settled anything.

HELMER Darling, that wasn't your way.

NORA That's it exactly. You've never understood me.   495
You've done me great wrong, Torvald – you, and
Daddy before you.

HELMER The two men who loved you most in all the
world?

NORA (*shaking her head*). You never loved me. Either of   500
you. It pleased you, that's all – the idea of loving me.

HELMER What are you telling me?

NORA The truth, Torvald. When I lived with Daddy, he
told me his views on everything, so I shared his views.
If I disagreed I didn't say so: he'd have hated it. He   505
called me his little dolly-baby, and played with me as I
played with my dollies. Then I came here, to you –

HELMER Is that how you describe our marriage?

NORA (*calmly*). I was transferred from Daddy's care to
yours. You organised everything to suit yourself: your   510
taste. So I shared your taste, or pretended to, I'm not
sure which. Perhaps both: sometimes one, sometimes
the other. I realise it now: I lived here hand to mouth,
like a beggar. I've existed to perform for you, Torvald.
That's what you wanted. You've done me great harm,   515
you and Daddy: you've blocked my life.

HELMER You're unreasonable, Nora, ungrateful. Haven't you been happy here?

NORA No, never. I thought I was, but I wasn't.

HELMER Not ... happy ... ? 520

NORA Cheerful. You've always been kind to me. But it's as if we live in a Wendy house. I'm your dolly-wife, just as I used to be Daddy's dolly-baby. And my dolls were the children. When you played with me, I had a lovely time – and so did they when I played with them. That's 525 our marriage, Torvald. That's what it's been like.

HELMER Maybe you're right. Hysterical, overwrought, but a little bit right. And now things are going to change. Playtime ends; lessons begin.

NORA Mine? Or the children's? 530

HELMER Darling, yours *and* theirs.

NORA Torvald, how could *you* ever teach me to be a proper wife? Your wife?

HELMER You're joking.

NORA And how could I ever teach the children? 535

HELMER Nora!

NORA You said so yourself just now. You'd never trust me again.

HELMER I'd lost my temper. Surely, you didn't think I 540 meant it?

NORA It was the truth. I can't bring them up. I've someone else to bring up first – myself. You can't help. I must do it myself. That's why I'm leaving you.

HELMER (*jumping up*). What?

NORA If I'm to come to terms with myself, understand 545 myself, I have to be alone. I can't stay here.

HELMER Nora, Nora.

NORA I'll go right away. I'll sleep at Kristine's tonight.

HELMER You're mad. I forbid this.

NORA No more forbidding. I'll take what belongs to me. I 550 need nothing of yours, either now or later.

HELMER You're out of your mind.

NORA Tomorrow I'll go home – I mean, where I was born.
I'll find something there.

HELMER You're blind. You don't know how – 555

NORA I'll find out how.

HELMER Deserting your home, your husband, your
children. What will people say?

NORA I must. Let them say what they like.

HELMER It's unbelievable. You abandon your most sacred 560
obligations –

NORA You know what they are, then, my sacred
obligations?

HELMER You need me to tell you? To your husband, your 565
children.

NORA I've other obligations, just as sacred.

HELMER Of course you haven't. What obligations?

NORA To myself.

HELMER You're a wife, a mother. They come first.

NORA I don't think so, now. Not any more. I think that 570
first I'm a human being, the same as you. Or at least
that I'll try to be one. I know that most people would
agree with you, Torvald, that that's what they teach in
books. But I've had enough of what most people say,
what they write in books. It's not enough. I must think 575
things out for myself, I must decide.

HELMER You should think about your place, here in your
own home. Have you nothing to guide you? No ...
belief?

NORA I don't know what that is. 580

HELMER What?

NORA All I know is what Pastor Hansen taught at
confirmation class. Belief is this, and this, he said. I'll
think about it, when I've time, when I've gone away.
Work out if Pastor Hansen's belief was right – for me. 585

HELMER You're a girl, a child! If belief doesn't affect you, what about conscience? Morality? Or have you none of that?

NORA I can't answer. I don't know. I'm baffled. All I know is, you and I have different ideas about it all. 590
And the law – I've discovered that's not what I always thought it was, and I can't believe it's right. A woman mustn't spare her dying father, or save her husband's life. I can't believe it.

HELMER You're talking like a child. You don't understand 595
the society you live in.

NORA You're right: I don't. But I'm going to find out – which of us is right, society or me.

HELMER Nora, you're ill. You're delirious. I think you're raving. 600

NORA I've never felt better. My mind's never been clearer.

HELMER Clearer? Leaving your husband, your children – ?

NORA That's what I'm doing.

HELMER There's only one explanation.

NORA What? 605

HELMER You've stopped loving me.

NORA That's it exactly.

HELMER How can you say that?

NORA It hurts, Torvald. You've always been wonderful to me. But I can't help it. I've just stopped loving you. 610

HELMER (*controlling himself*). Something else you're clear about?

NORA Completely clear. It's why I'm going.

HELMER And what did I do? To lose your love? Can you tell me that? 615

NORA It was tonight. The miracle didn't happen. I saw you weren't the man I'd imagined.

HELMER You're not making sense.

NORA For eight years I've waited patiently. Miracles don't happen every day, God knows. Then I was engulfed in 620 catastrophe, and I was certain: it'll happen now, the miracle. When Krogstad sent his letter, I was certain you'd never give in to him. You'd tell him to publish and be damned. And then –

HELMER When I'd exposed my own wife to disgrace and shame – ? 625

NORA Then, I was certain, you'd take the whole thing on your own shoulders, and say, 'I did it. I was the guilty one.'

HELMER Nora – ! 630

NORA You think I'd have denied it? Of course I would. But what would my word have been worth, compared with yours? That was the miracle I hoped for – and it was to prevent it that I was going to kill myself.

HELMER Darling, I'd work night and day for you. I'd 635 endure starvation, agony. But no man sacrifices his *honour* for the one he loves.

NORA Hundreds of thousands of women do just that.

HELMER You're talking – thinking – like a child.

NORA Perhaps. But you're not talking or thinking like the 640 husband I long for. As soon as you stopped panicking – not panicking for me, but for what might happen to you – when it was over, you behaved as if nothing at all had happened. So far as you were concerned, I went back to what I'd always been: your pet bird, your doll, 645 which you'd now have to treat with extra care because I was fragile, breakable. (*getting up.*) That's when I realised, Torvald. For eight years I've lived with a stranger. Borne him three children. I can't bear it. I'd like to tear myself to pieces. 650

HELMER (*heavily*). It's clear. It's clear. There's a gulf opened up between us. But surely we can bridge it, fill it?

NORA The woman I am now is no wife for you.

HELMER I'll change. I can change – 655

85

NORA If your doll's taken away, perhaps.

HELMER Nora. Don't leave me. I don't understand.

NORA That's why I must.

She goes into the room right, and comes back with her cloak and hat and a small suitcase, which she puts on the chair by the table.

HELMER Not tonight. Tomorrow.

NORA (*putting on her cloak*). I can't spend the night in a   660
strange man's house.

HELMER Brother and sister? Can't we live like that?

NORA (*putting on her hat*). It wouldn't last. You know
that.

She puts on the shawl.

Goodbye, Torvald. I don't want to see the children.   665
They're in better hands than mine. The woman I am
now can do nothing for them.

HELMER One day, Nora, one day – ?

NORA How can I answer? I don't know what I'll be.

HELMER Whatever you'll be, whatever you are, you're still   670
my wife.

NORA Torvald, listen to me. When a wife deserts her
husband, as I'm deserting you, the law frees him of all
obligations towards her. And in any case, I set you
free. You're not bound in any way. You're free. We're   675
both free. On both sides: freedom. Take back your
ring. Give me mine.

HELMER That too?

NORA That too.

HELMER There.   680

NORA Thankyou. It's over. I'll put the keys here. The
servants know where everything is – better than I do.
Tomorrow, as soon as I've left the town, Kristine will
come and pack my things – my own things, the things I
brought from home. I'll have them sent on.   685

HELMER Over. Over. Nora, won't you ever think of me?

NORA Often. You, the children, this house –

HELMER Can I write to you?

NORA No. It's forbidden.

HELMER I could send you –   690

NORA Nothing.

HELMER If you needed help –

NORA I'll take nothing from a stranger.

HELMER Will I never be more to you?

NORA (*taking the case*). If the miracle happened –   695

HELMER Tell me the miracle.

NORA If we changed, both of us, if we – No, Torvald. I've
stopped believing in miracles.

HELMER I believe. Tell me. If we changed, if we –

NORA If we discovered some true relationship. Goodbye.   700

> *She goes out through the hall.* HELMER *slumps into a
> chair by the door and covers his face.*

HELMER Nora! Nora!

> *He gets up, looks round.*

Empty. She's gone.

> *A hope flashes across his face.*

A miracle – ?

> *A door slams, off.*
> *Final Curtain.*

RESOURCE NOTES

Who has written *A Doll's House* and why?

The life of Henrik Ibsen

> *Everything that I have written is most minutely*
> *connected with what I have lived through, if not*
> *personally experienced.*

Henrik Ibsen was born on 20 March 1828 at Skien, a small town on the south-east coast of Norway, to a prosperous merchant family. He was the eldest of five children. Ibsen had a difficult childhood from the age of eight, as his father had many financial problems and the family suffered social embarrassment owing to their poverty. He later recalled how his father's friends deserted him as his social status changed and how his parents became withdrawn and bitter following their financial ruin. Another source of embarrassment for the young boy was the rumour that he was the illegitimate son of an old admirer of his mother's. There was little evidence to support this gossip but it affected him for many years.

Ibsen was educated at a small private school, where he worked hard and demonstrated his talent as a painter. He decided that he wanted to be a doctor, but the study of medicine would have been too expensive, and at fifteen he became assistant to an apothecary. There he was overworked, but he was also a determined young man and persevered with his studies throughout this difficult time. He preferred solitude to socialising and enjoyed reading theology and writing poetry.

During these years Ibsen began to resent the very inward-looking atmosphere of Skien, and decided to move to the capital, Christiania, now Oslo. Despite his continued efforts with his studies, Ibsen failed his university entrance examination. In 1850, his first play, *Catiline*, a historical verse drama, was rejected by the Christiania Theatre. Ibsen turned his attention to political affairs in this period and became active in the socialist movement.

In the early decades of the nineteenth century there was a nationalist revival in Norway. The country had been ruled by Denmark from 1397, but this subjugation ended in 1818. Literary figures and historians tried to show a connection with the heroic past of the middle ages; they wrote about historical events, hoping that this would inspire the Norwegian people. At the same time, the Romantic Movement was sweeping across Europe. Ole Bull, a successful violinist and composer, and a man with strong nationalist sentiments, founded a theatre in Bergen, with the expressed intention of promoting Norwegian culture. Ibsen, to his delight, was appointed dramatic author in 1851. Here he was able to gain the practical theatrical experience he needed: he wrote, directed, supervised the dialogue, designed sets, blocked scenes, stage managed, and kept financial books. He was also contracted to produce an original dramatic work for the second of January each year. This was a difficult task as he had insufficient time to develop his plays and consequently *The Warrior's Barrow* (1850) and *St John's Night* (1853) were considered dramatic failures; *Lady Inger of Ostraat* (1855) and *The Feast of Solhaug* (1856) were slightly more successful.

At the age of 28, Ibsen met the woman he was to marry, Suzannah Thoresen. She was well read, independent thinking and assertive, and she left her mark on Ibsen's strong-willed female characters such as Nora. Suzannah became a great source of strength to her husband, ensuring that he was never disrupted while working. They had one child, Sigurd, who was born in 1859.

In 1857, Ibsen left the Bergen Theatre to become artistic director of the Norwegian Theatre in Christiania. However, he had limited success in this role; his choice of plays was criticised by the media. The public did not seem interested in variety; instead they were content with light comedies and musical entertainment. Ibsen found this restricting and was consequently frustrated and disillusioned. There was no outlet for his creative abilities and he did not publish anything from 1857 to 1862. The theatre was doing badly, Ibsen's salary was reduced and he gradually fell into debt and began to drink heavily. In 1862, The Norwegian Theatre went bankrupt and he lost his livelihood. He also lost his faith in the power of nationalism, which had been the basis for his early work. From 1863 to 1864, Norway failed to give help to neighbouring Denmark when Prussia declared war. This angered Ibsen; his romantic belief in a modern Scandinavia that would recall a heroic past, was destroyed.

The latter years of Ibsen's life from 1864 were happier and more artistically fulfilling. *A Love's Comedy* (1863) and *The Pretenders* (1864) received favourable reviews, and Ibsen also wrote the highly successful verse allegories *Brand* (1866) and *Peer Gynt* (1867). After gaining a travelling scholarship, Ibsen went into self-imposed exile and did not return to Norway for 27 years. In Germany and Italy Ibsen felt inspired to write, now that he was free from the stultifying and reactionary environment that hampered his artistic development. Artistic success and an improvement in finances meant that he was able to look at more adventurous themes: in 1869 his play *The League of Youth* raised issues of class and power and threatened to question conventional values.

During the 1870s, there was a definite change in Ibsen's focus of interest. He moved from writing historical epics and verse allegories to a form of contemporary realism. His main interest was in social criticism and the use of colloquial, familiar, everyday language. He wanted to subject the values of the society in which he lived to close scrutiny and to draw attention to its defects. He had a desire to transform the individual from the limits imposed by social and political structures; he said, 'untruth does not reside in institutions but in the individuals themselves within the community' (Ibsen,

Brev by Øyvind Anker, p. 218). His later plays *The Pillars of Society* (1871) , *A Doll's House* (1879), *Ghosts* (1881) and *Hedda Gabler* (1890) were commercially successful, though controversial. Ibsen was a perfectionist and reworked and revised these plays with great care and attention. He kept to himself when he worked, expressing his need for solitude and isolation. In the 1890s, however, he became involved with Emilie Bardach, aged 18, the first of a series of liaisons with younger women.

Ibsen received critical acclaim for his work during his own lifetime and was awarded several honours, which he prized greatly. In 1891 he returned to Norway, the homeland where he had once felt so ill at ease, and died in 1906 after suffering several disabling strokes.

✦ *Activities*

1 Using these biographical notes and any other research you can do, consider how these events may have affected the composition of *A Doll's House.*

2 Think of reasons why Ibsen might have moved from writing historical epics and verse allegories to dramas of social realism with a more informal use of language. Look up each of these genres in the *Cambridge Guide to Literature in English* or in an encyclopaedia.

Historical background

Ibsen was strongly influenced by Norway's political situation. The political subjection to Denmark may have ended in 1814, but it was followed by an enforced union to Sweden until 1905. After gaining a constitution, Norway needed to build up a distinctive cultural identity, and writers looked to historical, mythological and folk stories to justify Norway's identity. In the 1850s, most of Ibsen's plays were based on historical and literary sources. He was later to realise that his hopes for a

Norwegian nationhood were unrealistic, and this led to a change in dramatic focus – an interest in the emerging middle classes of his time.

From 1814 onwards, free enterprise capitalism and increasing prosperity made Norwegian people financially comfortable, and therefore relatively optimistic. Business flourished and industrialisation made more consumer goods available. Acquiring capital and economic freedom led the bourgeois classes to defend the establishment, even though this went against their expressed ideals. Ibsen felt that the protected middle-class world prevented people from aspiring to greater things.

There were several political uprisings and revolutions in Europe in 1848. The discontent of the working classes had economic roots. The grievances of the middle classes were more political; they resented their exclusion from power and struggled for liberty and independence against established systems of government. Ibsen empathised with their situation. However, although the revolutions in Europe seemed liberating, middle-class individuals continued to conform to what society required. The benefits of a materialistic lifestyle encouraged them to be self-satisfied and complacent.

◆ Activities

1 Aim to find out more about the 1848 revolutions in Europe. Examine the causes and the motivations of those involved. Use photographs and illustrations of the period from books and magazines and construct a collage of what was happening at the time. Also attempt to find out about any particularly heroic figures.

2 Examine Nora's preoccupation with materialism and her extravagant spending habits in the early stages of the play, and then find key words and phrases that suggest her

concern with more spiritual issues and personal freedom in the third act.

Theatrical background

Ibsen's writing was deeply influenced by the theatrical developments of his time.

As Norway was still culturally influenced by Denmark for many years after 1814, it had no established theatrical tradition. In the 1790s, amateur travelling companies would tour Norwegian towns performing light comedies and musical routines. When the Christiania Theatre was opened in 1827, the acting of Norwegians was considered to be inferior to that of their neighbours, and so Danish actors were still employed in preference.

In the early nineteenth century, the so-called 'well-made plays' of Eugène Scribe (1791–1861), a French dramatist, were very popular, with their stock character types, predictable story lines and focus on dramatic intrigue. The plots were complex, full of misunderstandings and coincidences and the characters were required to act in melodramatic styles. Ibsen was later to criticise these plays as 'dramatic candyfloss'.

In the mid-nineteenth century, however, there was a reaction against these plays and a changing view about the function of the theatre. In an essay published in 1880, 'Naturalism in the Theatre', Emile Zola accused French and European drama of being 'mechanical, superficial, lacking in authentic characters and still perpetuating outworn clichés of romanticism'. The theatre was primarily there to provide entertainment and to support the values of prevailing social and political systems (Williams, *Ibsen and the Theatre 1877–1900*, pp. 165, 176). Several theatre practitioners felt that theatre should be considering the problems of the age, such as the effects of industrialisation.

Ibsen was also influenced in his ideas about the nature of modern drama by a German scholar called Hermann Hettner.

In *Das Moderne Drama*, Hettner said that social and historical plays should be relevant to modern times, characters should be well developed and that there was no use for the techniques of the 'well-made play'. Another inspiration for Ibsen was Sax Meiningen, whose ensemble of actors attempted to make their characters realistic and credible. Sets became an integral part of the performance, not mere decor to be overlooked. A theatre critic of the time explained how the company even took the trouble to distinguish between different types of trees on their sets!

Theatre practice in the early nineteenth century was governed by set rules and conventions on stage positioning, but there was a lack of direction; much was left to the discretion of the individual actor. Actors were positioned in horizontal rows and faced the audience even while speaking to each other. There were few rehearsals and directorial responsibilities were divided between two people. The sets had backdrops with paintings on them of furniture and properties, and for scenic changes, backdrops on castors were pushed on and off stage. Many objects were labelled and did not look realistic by modern-day standards. Pantomimes use similar devices to this day. Candles in chandeliers were used for lighting the stage, although in 1879, the year of *A Doll's House*, an important technological development took place with the invention of Edison's incandescent bulbs.

✦ *Activity*

Investigate how these rules and conventions compare with staging a play today. Each group in your class might research a different comparative aspect of the theatre then and today and do a presentation of its findings. If appropriate, use your history and drama departments to help you in your research.

Ibsen's influence on the theatre

Although Ibsen used traditional dramatic forms, he was also interested in symbolism and psychological depth of character. He was particularly keen to introduce new kinds of acting. Henry James noted, 'the opportunity that he gives them is almost always to do the deep and delicate thing' (*The Scenic Art*, pp. 253–254). The actors had more demands on them in his plays; there were no set rules and characters were not revealed chronologically as in conventional drama, but through memory, which is non-linear. His characters were no longer stereotypes, but combined complex, contradictory elements. Ibsen also reversed traditional gender roles in his plays; women in particular do not always behave in a predictably 'feminine' way, as shown by Nora in Act 3 of *A Doll's House*.

For Ibsen, stage setting became integral to the development of character. He was very precise about design and detail and the objects and the actions of the characters also had a symbolic significance, for example Nora's body language during the ritual dance of the victim of the tarantula spider.

Ibsen saw the importance of how dress reveals social and economic status and state of mind. One of the major themes of the play is masquerading; as Nora changes her costume it mirrors changes in her own development. She dresses up to please Torvald, but the dress also symbolises delusions in the doll's house. In Act 2, Nora expresses her repulsion and wants to tear up everything it represents. Eventually she attempts to restore it and resign herself to her situation.

✦ *Activities*

1 Look at the role of some of the stage 'props' in the play. Take the Christmas tree as an example. A tree is often seen as a symbol of life. It is also a cultural signifier, and in the 1870s it was a distinct status symbol. The critic Durbach sees it as a metaphor in the process of the transformation of Nora

(*A Doll's House: Ibsen's Myth of Transformation*, p. 53). In Act 1, Nora hides the tree and yet at the end of Act 1 it is in the focal position; by Act 2 the tree is disarranged. How might these movements and changes in its physical appearance reflect what is happening in the house?

In small groups consider the symbolic significance of other stage 'props' such as the macaroons, the stove or the lamp.

2 There are many references to doors: the play begins with the door opening and finishes with the door slamming. Doors shut and enclose; they can exclude you, but they can also serve to hide. Consider which doors are **not** opened in the course of the play and what this might suggest.

3 Design your own versions of the Christmas tree and Nora's costume. Try to achieve theatrical impact with your designs and ensure that both items are convincing possessions of the Helmers.

◆

The life of Henrik Ibsen (1828–1906)

1828	Henrik Ibsen born 20 March at Skien in Norway.
1834	Father's financial problems necessitate move to a smaller house.
1844	Becomes an assistant to an apothecary in Grimstad. He is overworked but continues his education for university.
1846	Illegitimate son born to Ibsen's mistress, a servant of the apothecary.
1849	*Cataline*, first romantic verse play, is rejected by the Christiania Theatre.
1850	Fails university entrance exam. Becomes involved in the socialist movement. First performance of *The Warrior's Barrow* in Christiania.
1851	Takes up appointment as dramatic author at the Norwegian Theatre in Bergen.
1852	Study tour to theatres in Hamburg, Copenhagen and Dresden.
1855	*Lady Inger of Oestraat*, a historical tragedy, performed at Bergen.
1856	*The Feast of Solhous* performed. Engaged to Suzannah Thoresen, a month after meeting her.
1857	Leaves Bergen to become artistic director of Norwegian Theatre in Christiania.
1858	Criticised for play choices and falls into debt.
1859	Son Sigurd born to his wife, Suzannah.
1862	Norwegian Theatre declared bankrupt and Ibsen loses job. *Love's Comedy* published.
1863	Becomes part-time literary adviser to Danish Christiania Theatre.
1863	Awarded a travel grant from the government and leaves Norway for 27 years.

1864	First performance of *The Pretenders* at Christiania Theatre.
	Settles in Rome.
1866	*Brand*, a verse allegory, published and well received.
1867	Successful publication of *Peer Gynt*.
1868	Travels extensively and goes to Dresden.
1869	*League of Youth*, a modern prose comedy, published.
1873	*Emperor and Galilean*, a historical epic, published.
1875	Returns to Norway after ten years, but soon moves abroad again to Munich.
1877	*The Pillars of Society*, Ibsen's first realist play, an immediate success.
1879	*A Doll's House* published and staged in Copenhagen. A great success in Scandinavia and Germany.
1880	Returns to Italy.
	The Pillars of Society, the first play to be performed in England, translated by William Archer.
1881	*Ghosts* published, amid controversy.
1882	First performance of *A Doll's House* in English.
	An Enemy of the People published.
1884	*The Wild Duck* published.
1885	Second visit to Norway in twenty years; moves from Rome to Munich.
1886	Censors forbid the public performance of *Ghosts*.
1888	*The Lady from the Sea* published.
1890	Becomes involved with Emilie Bardach, aged 18; the first of a series of sexual liaisons with younger women.
	First collection of Ibsen's drama in English. *Hedda Gabler* published to unfavourable reviews.

1890	G. B. Shaw delivers lecture on Ibsen to Fabian Society.
1891	London premiere of *Ghosts*. Returns to Norway to live.
1892	Publication of *The Master Builder*.
1894	*Little Eyolf* published.
1896	*John Gabriel Borkman* published. Receives several honours.
1899	*When We Dead Awaken* published
1900–01	Suffers several strokes and is left paralysed.
1906	23 May: Ibsen dies, aged 78.

◆

What type of text is *A Doll's House*?

A translation

The play in this edition has been translated by Kenneth McLeish. *A Doll's House* was originally written in Riksmal, the official language of the church and state, which was later absorbed into Norwegian. The play has been translated into many languages. One of the difficulties of translation is in getting the colloquial feel and subtleties of everyday speech conveyed appropriately in another language. An obvious example occurs at the end of one translation of the play. Nora says she was never happy, 'just gay'. There are occasions when the two words 'happy' and 'gay' could be used to mean the same thing today, but 'gay' now also means 'homosexual', a meaning it did not have in Ibsen's time.

In Michael Meyer's 1985 translation, Nora says she was never 'happy', but just 'had fun'. In McLeish's version, Nora was just 'cheerful'. In Riksmal, the equivalent *Lykkelig* and *lystig* signify very different emotions, and the subtleties of the difference can be lost in translation. The critic Durbach suggests that 'happy' is meant to represent a spiritual condition of well-being here, and 'gay' and 'fun' have associations with something temporary, like lust or desire. We have to be aware that, at times, expressions from the original can have meanings that are lost.

Nora, in some English translations, has a desire to say 'damn' or 'bloody hell'. McLeish translates it as 'good God'. This may not seem very amazing to a modern audience, but Durbach translates the line precisely for us: *Jeg har sådar es umådelig lyst tilat sige: **død og pine***; she really wants to cry out in 'death and pain', a comment on her suffering. In 1879, an audience would have been shocked by this, but it may lose some of its impact in the present climate, when expletives and swear words are used more readily.

It is illuminating to compare different translations, as they can lead to quite different productions. Think about some of the differences between McLeish's and Meyer's translations. Our initial impressions of Nora are created before she says anything: Meyer has her 'humming contentedly', but in McLeish's text she is 'happy humming a tune'. The director will have to interpret these, and there will be a difference in how the humming is portrayed.

Another example occurs in Act 1, when Nora attempts to hide the macaroons. She 'puts' one in her mouth in McLeish's translation, 'pops' one in her mouth in Meyer's version, and J. W. McFarlane uses the word 'stuffs'. If each of these gestures is acted out you will find that they create different impressions of Nora's character. Her concealment would be portrayed differently depending on the version you had access to.

◆ Activities

1 Try to get hold of a translation by Michael Meyer or J. W. McFarlane. In small groups, compare and contrast different sections and report your findings back to the whole class for discussion.

2 In McLeish's edition, Nora is portrayed as 'rustling' like a squirrel; McFarlane uses 'frisking'. What different implications do these words have for her character?

3 In McLeish's translation, Nora suggests in her conversation with Kristine Linde that Torvald 'earns a lot of money'; Meyer's version has 'makes a lot of money'. What connotations does the verb 'make' have? What type of financial power has Torvald got? Does Nora see him as a creator, in any way?

Genre

A Doll's House is difficult to classify as belonging to any one particular genre. It could be seen as a modern tragedy, a 'well-made play', a melodrama or a realistic problem drama. Each of these is investigated below.

Modern tragedy

Ibsen called the play 'a tragedy of the contemporary age', so it is modern, and yet it is similar in some respects to the classical form. In traditional tragedy, a tragic flaw, transgression or excess of arrogant ambition leads to the downfall of a heroic individual and this is treated in a serious and dignified style. The ordeal is not wholly negative, as we see a new side to the protagonist. Ibsen was credited as the first major dramatist to write tragedy about ordinary people in prose. He deals with painful contemporary situations and explores individual frustration and inadequacy. The protagonist becomes the victim of the restrictions and the corrupt nature of a society s/he tries to react or protest against. *A Doll's House* is the tragedy of a Norwegian housewife who is forced to challenge law and society, and her husband's value system. She gives up her roles as wife and mother and reclaims herself, but in the process she is isolated after years of social conditioning. She has to confront suffering as she gains insight into her self.

✦ Activities

1 In groups, find the points in the play where Nora confronts an illusion, and those moments when she seems to be deprived of support, for example when she realises that she is under a misapprehension in thinking Torvald will sacrifice everything for her.

2 Using these brief notes and any other research you are able to do on modern tragedy, discuss in what ways Nora is a modern tragic heroine.

3 In *Death of a Salesman* (1949), Arthur Miller extends Ibsen's concept of tragedy. A young travelling salesman tragically accepts the false values of contemporary society. If you have

time, try to read this play and compare Willy Loman's predicament with Nora's.

Well-made play

Eugène Scribe (1791–1861) said, 'You go to the theatre for relaxation and amusement, not for instruction or correction'. His well-made plays had very artificial constructions: suspenseful revelations, detailed expositions and coincidences. There would always be a climax in the action followed by a reversal of expectations due to a revelation from the past. Eventually, there would be a satisfactory resolution and the 'status quo' would be restored. Ibsen, however, wanted the audience to bring its conscience to the theatre and become actively involved in the theatrical process. George Bernard Shaw has shown, in *The Quintessence of Ibsen*, how the traditional well-made play with exposition, situation and unravelling was replaced by Ibsen with a complication, and a discussion of the issues raised. He left out the reconciliation, although his plays looked as though they were going to be conventional. Krogstad, for instance, may seem like a villain, but he has redeeming characteristics and is capable of change.

✦ Activities

1 Consider the ways in which Ibsen uses elements from the well-made play in *A Doll's House*.

2 Discuss what issues are **not** resolved at the end of the play.

Melodrama

Melodrama was very popular in the nineteenth century. Traditionally, the plays had plots and characters that were exaggerated for effect. Some of the key elements of melodrama were:

- expressive emotional gestures conveying excitement or agitation;

- disjointed styles of speech, rather like the register of telegrams;
- self-dramatising, and suicidal fantasies;
- stock characters, totally good or bad, and ideas divided simply into rights and wrongs;
- sensational events;
- overblown language to convey the extreme emotions.

✦ *Activity*

Look at some of Nora's responses to her situation, and at Krogstad's language. Does Ibsen incorporate any melodramatic elements? Are they ever criticised or undermined by the dramatist in the context in which they appear?

Realistic problem drama

Ibsen was keen to move away from the genre of romantic drama, where life is presented as we would like to have it – more adventurous and more heroic. Instead, he strove to present objective reality:

> It takes a more powerful vision to glimpse things which are artistically usable amid all the chance events one is caught up in, than it does to detect them, for example, in a past age, which stands at a distance.
>
> (Bjørn Hemmer, 'Ibsen and the Realistic Problem Drama', 1994)

Émile Zola was one of the early exponents of realist literature, which was supposed to 'represent reality truthfully'. The defining characteristics of realism were social 'problems' (such as marriage, religion, property rights and the relations between the sexes) and a critical perspective. *A Doll's House* was a modern realistic drama, challenging the values of the conservative middle-class Victorian society with its façade of false morality. 'Reality' meant the impression of the world which the reader/audience and the writer had in common.

However, we need to be aware that this concept presents difficulties. For example, which and whose reality are we talking about? Does each of us have our own sense of reality? One view is that reality is constructed in the mind, although the mind can think that reality is independent of it.

In realistic problem dramas, the individual is often in opposition to a hostile society. Ibsen was aware that as a social critic he was responsible as a member of that society, but he tried to reveal its defects. In *A Doll's House*, the bourgeois family is seen to be a microcosm of the hierarchical power structure of the larger social, financial and legal worlds.

◆ *Activities*

1 Look at some of the repressive attitudes in society towards things that threaten the 'status quo' in *A Doll's House*. How do these compare with those in the present day?

2 Look at the ways in which Torvald adapts to what society requires of him, and how he defends society's structures and the family. What destabilising threats are there to this society and what are its control mechanisms?

3 Ibsen was a man of his times. Do some research on some thinkers who may have influenced his writing. Use your library resources to discover more about Darwin and scientific naturalism, Brandes, Hegel and Kierkegaard. See if you find any similarities between their ideas and the ideas raised in *A Doll's House*.

How was *A Doll's House* produced?

Ibsen worked to tight deadlines and liked to work in isolation, finding social life stultifying when he was trying to get ideas for his plays. Before he began to write, he would meditate: 'before I write I must know the character through and through'. Henrik Jaegar, Ibsen's first biographer, shows that Ibsen's working methods indicate a disparity between 'brooding time', which took eighteen months, and active writing, which took six months (McFarlane, *The Cambridge Companion to Ibsen*, pp.162–163). He was very methodical in refining work in the later years.

The inspiration for *A Doll's House* came from the tragic events that happened to Laura Kieler, a young woman Ibsen met in 1870. She asked Ibsen to comment on a play she was writing and they became close friends. Some time later her husband contracted tuberculosis and was advised to visit a warm climate. Unfortunately, they lacked the financial means, so she acquired a loan. Repayment was demanded and Laura had to forge a cheque. This was soon discovered and her husband treated her like a common criminal, despite the fact that she had taken these actions for his sake. She suffered a nervous breakdown and was committed to a public asylum. Eventually, she begged him to take her back for the sake of the children. Unfortunately, *A Doll's House* was resented by the woman who had inspired it.

A Doll's House was performed in the municipal theatres throughout Germany immediately after the premiere in the Royal Theatre, Copenhagen on 4 December 1879. It was a great success but, despite its popularity, the ending had to be rewritten and the original 'unsuitable' version left out. Audiences objected to the fact that a woman could desert her children so readily. In the German edition of the third act, Nora does not leave home, for the sake of the children. Torvald drags her to the bedroom door. She lets the bags drop to the floor and says, 'Oh this is a sin against myself, but I cannot leave them'. Torvald offers her a macaroon as she says, 'the miracle of miracles'. Ibsen called the rewrite 'a barbaric outrage', and said that it should only be used in emergencies. There was no popular or critical consensus about Ibsen's plays, and perhaps this was his intention. As Simon Williams says: 'The polemics of Ibsen's drama divided the audience and revealed rather than covered the broader rifts within society as a whole' (*Ibsen and the Theatre 1877–1900*, p. 171).

✦ Activities

1 In the early drafts, the child characters were given individual lines to say, but Ibsen gradually left the lines out and they became 'children'. What practical and artistic reasons do you think there were for this decision?

2 Write your own alternative ending to the play, in which Nora returns to the family. After writing, hold a class discussion on which type of ending is more satisfactory.

✦

How is *A Doll's House* presented?

Ibsen was motivated by his desire to write about moral conflicts and the clash that can arise between what a person is able to do and what he or she aspires to do. The Christian church was no longer seen as the sole authority telling people how to conduct their lives, and many believed they had suffered under powerful regimes for too long. Ibsen felt that people should strive to free their minds from the predetermining influences of heredity and environment. One way of achieving this would be to distance oneself from the establishment, but Ibsen realised that this could make the individual feel lonely and isolated.

The following concerns are intermingled in the text and should not be seen as separate 'subjects':

Moral conflict

One of Ibsen's major concerns is moral conflict and the dangers of deception. Before writing the play, Ibsen made the following note:

> There are two kinds of moral laws, two kinds of conscience, one for men and one quite different for women ... woman is judged by masculine law.

He also added that Nora loses faith in her own morality as her natural feelings and belief in authority come into conflict.

Torvald sees himself as a guardian of public morality as he affirms 'a stench of lies and deceit poisons the whole household'. He wishes to see his home as a stronghold of moral values and is protected from the harsher realities of the financial world. His reputation and social esteem are important to him, but Ibsen undermines this at points in the play. Personal and public morality come into conflict, for example when Torvald states, 'No man can sacrifice his honour for the one he loves', and later, 'you don't understand how society works'. In Act 3, Torvald ignores Nora's plea for forgiveness to make a moral judgement.

Several of the characters deceive themselves and those around them. Ibsen examines the link between deceit and role-playing or masquerading. One of Nora's first words in the play is 'hide', and we soon learn how skilled she is at concealment. There are many occasions when she lies or misrepresents the truth. In the eyes of the law, she is seen to be a criminal, forging her father's signature in order to get money for Torvald, but she says, 'I did it for love'. Krogstad replies, 'the law's not interested in reasons', and those reasons become 'a silly excuse' to Torvald. The play asks us to consider what Nora's motivation is, and whether avoiding the truth is ever justifiable or acceptable.

✦ Activities

1 At the end of Act 3, Kristine Linde says, 'The secret must come out. No more lies, tricks, they must understand each other'. Where are your sympathies at this point?

2 Examine the differences between private and public morality in the world of the play and the world now. Compare Krogstad's disgrace with the downfall of prominent politicians in recent years. What is considered unacceptable behaviour for a leading government minister? How does society treat those who offend its sensibilities? Look at the media attention given to such events.

3 Have attitudes to borrowing and debt changed, and if so, why? Is there anything wrong with charging interest? Are there hypocrisies in social attitudes towards money today?

Fate and free will

In the nineteenth century, there was concern about whether lives were shaped by our own free choice, or determined by a combination of our past, heredity and environment. In 1859,

Charles Darwin's *On the Origin of the Species* advanced the theory that animals and humans evolved according to the laws of natural selection; it was hugely influential. In *A Doll's House*, Ibsen considers genetic inheritance, congenital disease, the transmission of moral corruption and parental influence. Dr Rank is diseased owing to his father's indulgent life; his illness shows the inner corruption of a society that ignores its own problems. All of the characters are portrayed as socially conditioned, without the power of self-determination. Torvald is formed by social codes and conventions, and believes in the inevitable forces of heredity, saying for example that Nora's frivolity with money is inherited from her father, 'it's in your blood'.

In *A Doll's House*, Ibsen explores free will and how authority can inhibit its development. He also examines personal responsibility. As Nora moves out of her social context, and faces change, we see the human capacity to transform. She tries to discover who she is and undergoes a revolution of the human spirit. Ibsen is concerned with the necessity of liberating oneself from within.

✦ *Activity*

Make a list of all the conditions viewed as inescapable in the play. How would having a deterministic viewpoint affect your own life?

Gender

Simone de Beauvoir, the French author and feminist, once said, 'one isn't born a woman, one becomes one'. She meant, of course, that we all learn how to be a woman or a man as we grow up. According to this thinking, the gender terms 'feminine' and 'masculine' are social constructs, in other words, patterns of behaviour and sexuality imposed upon us by our culture and society, while 'female' and 'male' are used to denote the biological, sexual features we are all born with.

Many feminist critics have argued that, although all women are female, there is no inherent reason why they should be 'feminine'. For example, Nora is seen as unnatural for failing to play the roles of mother and wife, and Torvald asserts that it is natural for women to be primarily concerned with 'little things'. Ibsen has been praised and criticised for his sympathy with the feminist cause; he requires the audience to judge the actions and words of the characters in order to learn something about their own values. The female characters in Ibsen's plays are often seen to be limited by the rules and conventions of a male-dominated world, and by the requirement to be feminine. They are restricted by the roles of wife, mother, daughter and lover, and are rarely permitted to act independently. They are also stereotyped as seductress, femme fatale and manipulator. Ibsen was concerned about the effect such restricting roles could have:

> These women of the modern age, mistreated as daughters, as sisters, as wives, not educated according to their talents, debarred from following their missions, deprived of their inheritance, embittered in mind – these are the ones who supply the mothers for the new generation. What will be the result?

Nora, of course, challenges these conventional roles.

✦ Activities

1 Make a list of the advantages and disadvantages of getting married from the point of view of:
   - a woman living at the time when *A Doll's House* was set, and;
   - a woman today.

   What is meant by the 'double standard' in marriage?

2 Think about how a twentieth-century audience would react to Nora's abandonment of her children. Imagine that Nora leaves an explanatory letter. Write your version of the letter,

giving her reasons for leaving the children, and then write a reply to it from the point of view of a twentieth-century reader.

3 Society has developed a whole series of 'masculine' and 'feminine' characteristics. Feminine ones include sweetness, passivity, modesty, subservience and irrationality. Make a list of those you can find operating in *A Doll's House*. What are the equivalent masculine characteristics?

The language of the play

At the world premiere of *A Doll's House*, the Danish playwright Eric Boegh said that there was 'not a single declamatory phrase, no high dramatics, every needless line is cut, every exchange carries the action a step forward' (Non Worral, *A Doll's House*, p. 26).

Ibsen has been lauded for his creation of credible, realistic dialogue. It is worth looking at two twentieth-century plays where playwrights have tried to create such dialogue: *The Homecoming* by Harold Pinter and *Top Girls* by Caryl Churchill.

The language of Pinter's characters is naturalistic, with mumbling repetition, colloquial grammar, incomplete sentences, non sequiturs and sudden shifts of subject matter. People very often evade communication or fail to express themselves. Churchill employs the original device of overlapping dialogue in which speakers interrupt and continue speaking right through each other's speech.

In *A Doll's House*, all characters have habits of speech appropriate to their class and personality, but their individual voices are quite distinct. Much is revealed about the characters and their relationships through the language that they use.

Relationships

We define and understand Torvald and Nora's relationship through their language. Torvald uses labels and neologisms (made-up terms), when referring to Nora: 'skylark', 'squirrel', 'songbird' and 'featherbrain', and certain parallels can be drawn by observing her actions. Nora even appears to accept such definitions, 'songbirds, squirrels, you know how we spend'. People in intimate relationships often have terms of endearment for each other, creating fantasy worlds and alternative realities. The names that Torvald gives Nora could be seen as endearments, and yet he could also be objectifying her, trapping her in a destructive image. Torvald often teases Nora in a register you might not expect a husband to use with his wife, 'Nora, what have I here!'

Nora's language

Nora's language is genteel, indicating her social status, and is often tentative and careful, 'Now, shall I tell you what we ought to do?' This reveals a great deal about the nature of Nora's decisions. When Kristine Linde first arrives, Nora uses short phrases and seems impatient. Her verbosity and exhortations – 'Oh my poor', 'Oh fiddle', 'poor Kristine' – are quite different to Mrs Linde's pared-down lines, and they indicate her agitation. Nora is often exuberant, repeating certain words: Helmer has 'heaps of money', 'a big salary', 'lots of bonuses', 'lots and lots'. These vague, qualifying adjectives suggest her knowledge of financial affairs is limited. Nora changes her tone of language during this conversation, indicating that women speak in a different idiom when they are out of the company of men.

Torvald's language

Torvald uses many commands and imperatives when addressing Nora. When she asks him to look at her shopping purchases, Meyer's translation decides to put the focus of attention on Nora, 'You mustn't disturb me', while McFarlane translates the line as 'I don't want to be disturbed'. McLeish's version suggests that Torvald is more understanding, with the expression 'just a moment'. Torvald generally attempts to maintain the 'status quo'. In contrast to Nora, he is self-important, lecturing her with aphorisms and clichés: 'When a household relies on debts, it's slavery, it's vile.'

Minor characters

Krogstad's language shows his legal training, and also has a melodramatic element. He uses metaphors and imagery associated with shipwrecks, and in referring to Nora's suicide, he says: 'Under the ice perhaps? In the deep dark depths? Floating up in the spring, bloated, unrecognisable, your hair fallen out.'

Dr Rank also uses many figures of speech, including financial imagery to refer to his body: 'my poor blameless spine has to pay the bill'. He is unable to speak more explicitly about his father's sexual indiscretion and he is often convoluted in his expression: 'I shall avail myself of that privilege' (Meyer), 'you know that the dissolution, the vileness has begun' (McLeish). He also has a tendency to be dramatic. Kristine Linde's language contrasts with Dr Rank's; she does not use ornate language but speaks directly and concisely.

Imagery

There are many rich recurrent images in the play, where Ibsen suggests an alternative meaning beneath that which is literally stated. For example, there are references to the world of pretence and make-believe, and there are also images from the world of nature juxtaposed with those from the world of social conventions and bureaucracy.

✦ Activities

1 Explore the various ways in which Nora uses language to manipulate and persuade. Find key words and phrases she uses to influence Torvald.

2 Analyse the language Nora uses with her children; for example, she compares them with little red apples and roses. What else does she comment upon?

3 Nora's language changes as her interpretation of the world alters; her language is pared down considerably to monosyllables and simply formed statements: 'I'll leave the keys', 'thousands of women do just that', 'No more fancy dress'. What does this suggest?

4 Make up a soundtrack on a tape of some of the things Torvald has said to Nora in the past. Listen to this carefully, then analyse the defining characteristics of his speech.

✦ Extension activities

1 The language of characters is determined not only by their social class but also by their gender. Examine whether there is a masculine way of speaking, and whether this is different from a feminine way. For example, you might look at their main topics of conversation, or the styles in which men and women speak.

2 Imagine that Torvald, Nora, Krogstad and Kristine meet up again in ten years' time and write the script for this scene. Remember to indicate pauses and silences in the dialogue and try to capture the nuances of their speech.

Characterisation

Physical signs

One of the of the most interesting things about the characters is how they are revealed through their actions and contact with the objects around them. For example, Nora cannot express her anxiety adequately in speech, but she exorcises this through the tarantella dance. At certain moments in the play she moves towards the stove, and these actions perhaps convey her need for emotional warmth. A great deal is also revealed through the gestures of the characters. Nora puts her hand over her mouth, claps her hands frequently, jumps up, tosses her head and walks around the room. All of these gestures reveal a certain state of mind, and some have traditional associations.

✦ Activities

1 As a role-play exercise, choose different characters from the play and invent typical gestures or movements for them. Act these out and try to guess each other's characters.

2 Some gestures are used less regularly as the play progresses, for example the handclapping. What explanation can you find for Ibsen's decision here?

3 The exits and entrances of characters are significant. Compare the entrances of Krogstad, Kristine Linde and Torvald. What do they reveal about their characters? Think of Nora's state of mind as she says her last lines, and work out how she exits, concentrating on the exact impression you wish to create for an audience.

Nora

There are many different aspects to Nora's character. Look at her impulsive frivolous behaviour, her infantilism, mood swings, evasions, self-deceptions and the way in which she romanticises and ignores reality. Then consider her rational behaviour, practicality, astuteness, self-awareness and the way that she faces up to her responsibilities. She is an ambiguous character, with inconsistent moods, particularly in Act 1. We are constantly forced to reassess her in the light of new information, as Ibsen delineates character by suggestion rather than explanation.

The inner psychology of Nora is emphasised as she undergoes a transformation during the drama. She plays different roles, predetermined by society – the supportive wife, sexual being and mother – but at times Nora defies our expectations, particularly in her growing understanding of Torvald and the oppressive nature of her roles. She does not always see herself as subservient as she initially appears: 'We – that Torvald, has power over so many people.'

✦ Activities

1 Look at Nora's growing self-awareness, and consider the fluctuations in her emotional state as she changes. Draw a graph which plots the emotional temperature of the dialogue. Refer to the line in the text on the horizontal axis; use the vertical axis to plot the emotional temperature from calm to intense.

2 Read the lines from 'Torvald! What are you doing ...' (p. 74) to 'Goodbye' (p. 87). In pairs, one of you should play Nora and the other her conscience. Then write a dramatic soliloquy or diary entry to capture Nora's hopes and dreams for the future.

Torvald

Torvald may be seen as a respectable nineteenth-century husband. He has the dominant position in the household, and a subordinate woman sustains his ego. He can appear authoritarian and self-assured, concerned more with appearances than reality, confident in his support of social, religious and moral codes of the time. His arrogance means that he is dismissive of other characters in the play. However, there are also moments in the play where he seems imperceptive and weak, and in many ways he is a victim of the society in which he lives.

✦ Activities

1 You are given the chance to write a last speech for Torvald. What would he say?

2 Imagine that Torvald seeks to find a replacement for Nora. Write a profile on him for a dating agency and list his requirements. Compare your impressions with those of other students.

3 One perspective is to see Torvald as a respectable man who is nearly humiliated by a misguided wife. Can you find textual evidence to support this view?

Minor characters

Parallelism and juxtaposition are important strategies in the play, as we can learn more about one character through comparison with another. Nora and Anne-Marie are similar in that they both relinquish their children, but there are differences in what they eventually do: Anne-Marie accepts her destiny while Nora finally rejects hers.

Krogstad has many elements of the villain, yet he simply requires a socially respectable position like Torvald. Do you find your response alters towards him at all during the course of the play? In some ways he is persecuted by a harsh society, yet he exploits the system that nearly destroys him. There is an affinity between him and Nora as they commit the same crime, and yet Ibsen also makes us aware of their different motivations.

Ethical and physical degeneration are explored through the character of Dr Rank. He is a bitter and rather self-centred man, who sees society as determined, like his condition.

◆ *Activities*

1 The playwright George Bernard Shaw said that Torvald, not Krogstad, turns out to be the real villain. What evidence is there to suggest that this is so?

2 In groups, explore the conflicts between husband and wife by carrying out a role-play exercise in the form of a chat show on husbands and wives. Interview the four main characters as your special guests, and compare the alliance between Kristine Linde and Krogstad with that of Nora and Torvald.

3 Imagine that you are a psychiatrist. Write a report of Dr Rank's behaviour based on his language, his actions and what others have said about him.

4 In pairs, give sincerity ratings for each of the characters at different points in the play, on a scale from +5 (very sincere) to –5 (very insincere). Put your results on a chart and discuss your findings with those of other pairs.

5 As a large group activity, ask four volunteers to take on the roles of the main characters. Other students should submit questions that they would like to put to the characters if they were to stand trial to defend their actions in the play. Each will need a lawyer to act as support. The questions should be seen in advance, so that the characters have time to prepare their defence.

The dramatic structure

You may bring assumptions to the play about how the structure works depending on the plays you have seen, and to a certain extent on popular culture – films, soap operas and the conventions which govern them.

Plot

A Doll's House broadly follows the classical unities of form which were described by the Greek philosopher Aristotle (384–322BC). It is all set in the same place for seventy hours with a main and a minor plot. This unity of place strengthens the sense of confinement.

There are two elements from the 'well-made' play genre in *A Doll's House*: the focal letter-box, and the delayed leaving of Nora, both used to create tension. Our expectations are thwarted as the audience believes that Nora may find a miracle, Kristine Linde will influence Krogstad, or Krogstad will return the letter. However, for Ibsen there are no easy solutions and he concludes with a complication, leading to a discussion of the issues raised.

Retrospective technique

Ibsen uses the retrospective technique to reveal character and situation: action begins before Nora's plan is finished and the dialogue reveals events that took place previously. They are not literally presented. The first two acts are devoted to revelations. As the playwright Arthur Miller has said of such a technique, 'we are constantly aware of a process of change … the contrast between past and present and an awareness of the process by which the present has become what it is' (*Ibsen and the Drama of Today*). One of the revelations is that Nora did not spend time making trivial decorations, but stayed up at night copying to make money. She initially seems extravagant, for example when she gives the porter a hundred per cent tip, but the audience has continually to reassess her in the light of new information: evidence challenges evidence. There is an initial implication that Nora acquired money from an admirer, and we expect a sexual triad, but again Ibsen defies our expectations. The early events, however, do often anticipate later actions, if we remain alert to them. For example, Nora fears her daughter's cradle and doll will 'soon be broken', and this mirrors her own actions at the end.

Ibsen's use of dramatic irony is powerful: Torvald advises Kristine, for example, to 'always make a good exit, Mrs Linde – that's what I keep telling her'. He also refers to Nora's 'little secrets' that will 'all come out this evening'. He is of course unaware of the gravity of these, and the effects they will have.

✦ Activities

1 What Ibsen omits is as significant as what he chooses to include. Consider what is represented on and off stage. Why do you think the children rarely appear, and why are their responses not audible? Why is the fancy-dress ball not represented on stage?

2 Look at the different openings of each act. How do they set the mood for each scene? Make up a group tableau that captures the meaning of the final lines of Acts 1, 2 and 3. Produce captions or cartoons to capture the essence of each tableau.

✦

Who reads *A Doll's House*, and how do they interpret it?

It is helpful to consider your own reading of the text and where this comes from. The images you acquire as you read will be coloured by your existing experience and cultural preconceptions. An atheist, for example, would be likely to read a religious poem very differently from a Christian. There are many ways of reading *A Doll's House*; by way of example it is worth considering, briefly, two possible perspectives – a feminist reading and a Marxist reading.

A feminist reading

Feminist critics such as Kate Millett see gender and sexuality as central themes in literature; they also consider women to be oppressed to varying degrees in a male-dominated society. Although Ibsen denied taking up the feminist cause, he admitted supporting the concept of equality between the sexes:

> I must disclaim the honour of having consciously worked for the women's rights movement … to me it has been a question of human rights.
>
> (notes made for *A Doll's House*, 1878)

A feminist reading would suggest that *A Doll's House* offers a critique of the idea of motherhood as women's destiny. In many of Ibsen's plays, women are forced to give up their children or they desert them. Nora exchanges the limiting definition of the role of the mother for freedom; she rejects the division between conventional masculine and feminine behaviour and questions her duty to her husband and children as dictated by religion and society. According to a feminist reading, women who refuse motherhood are seen as abnormal. There are other dangers for the non-conforming woman: for example, Nora wishes to say 'good God', and Dr Rank's response is 'Tut, tut', an attempt to silence her. In Meyer's translation, Dr Rank says that the use of such language would suggest she's 'mad'; non-conforming behaviour may be interpreted by men as insanity.

✦ *Activities*

1 Ibsen's female figures have properties of the 'new woman', a literary type in Victorian fiction in the 1890s. The new woman valued independence and equality over self-sacrifice. Aim to discover more about this type. Gail Cunningham's *The New Woman and the Victorian Novel* (1978) is very helpful.

2 In what ways do the women capitulate to the social and sexual roles put upon them by male fantasy? Look at the text for examples of when Nora acquiesces to Torvald's power. Why might she do this? Virginia Woolf, in *A Room Of One's Own*, stated:

> Women have served all these centuries as looking glasses, possessing the magic and delicious power of reflecting the power of man at twice its natural size.

In what ways could Nora be described as Torvald's looking glass? Does she ever mirror his attitudes and tastes, or attempt to protect his image?

3 Improvise a secret meeting of the Norwegian Women's Liberation Group in Nora's town. Your task is to compile a charter listing demands for greater freedom for women.

A Marxist reading

Marxists emphasise the socio-economic element in any society as determining that society's character, so that social relationships are created by the methods of economic production employed in a society. In a capitalist society, the relationship between a capitalist and worker is founded on the capitalist exploiting the workforce, and thus is a relationship of conflict. The basic economic structures give rise to institutions and beliefs that keep that economic production going. Under a capitalist economy, these might be parliament, law courts and education systems. They are all geared to keeping values in place which uphold these institutions and the needs of capitalist production. Marx referred to this as the superstructure, and Marxist views of society emphasise the oppressions caused by the class of bourgeois capitalists, and their effect upon the class of workers, who are seen as virtuous but exploited.

Marxists see the struggle that Ibsen was demonstrating in *A Doll's House* as class-based rather than gender-based, and the play has been interpreted by Marxist critics as showing how the capitalist system corrupts human behaviour and relationships. Nora's predicament can be read as a metaphor for the oppression and exploitation of labour under the tyranny of capitalist man. Women and men are both seen as captive in this oppressive capitalist bourgeois society.

✦ *Activities*

1 How is your reading of *A Doll's House* affected by your position as a reader well over a century after it was written? Consider the fall of Communism in Europe and the revival of free enterprise. How might this affect a reading of the text?

2 In what ways is the capitalist financial system seen to corrupt human relationships in the play?

3 Aim to do some research on what life would have been like in Victorian times for the poorer classes. Where do you think Ibsen is directing our sympathies on the issue of class?

Producing the play

A stage production is also a 'reading' of the play. Directors have to interpret the stage directions and information provided by Ibsen; there is no definitive production but many performance choices.

For a director today, the contemporary social context in the play has now become the historical past, and this obviously affects interpretation. On the twentieth-century stage, modernists have found alternatives to the realistic style, and there has been a new approach to the staging of Ibsen. Instead of complex naturalistic details, they have used visual motifs to represent inner worlds behind the surface world. The modernists felt that some things were obviously more significant than others in a stage production and that these things should be emphasised and made explicit.

As early as the 1906 St Petersburg production, the director Vsevolod Meyerhold used a stylised set with a decrepit piano, a dilapidated three-legged stool, inconspicuous chairs, red drapes and a suspended window. He was attempting to show how uncomfortable and stultifying life was in 'the doll's house' and sought to present a strong visual image of Nora's inner life (Frederick and Lise Lone Marker, 'Ibsen and the Twentieth Century Stage', p. 188).

✦ Activity

You are a director about to stage the play. Who would you choose for your actors? Choose anyone you think suitable – public figures, film, rock or sports stars or fellow students. Say why you have cast people in particular roles. Then design a stage set to demonstrate your mental picture of the atmosphere and setting of A Doll's House. Aim to capture the status and the predicament of the Helmers.

✦

FURTHER READING

Chopin, K., *The Awakening* (Cambridge University Press, 1996)

Cunningham, G., *The New Woman and the Victorian Novel* (1978)

Churchill, C., *Top Girls* (Methuen, 1982)

Durbach, E., *A Doll's House: Ibsen's Myth of Transformation* (Twayne's Masterwork Studies, 1984)

Durbach, E. (ed.), *Ibsen and the Theatre* (Macmillan, 1980)

Egan, M. (ed.), *Ibsen: The Critical Heritage* (Routledge and Kegan Paul, 1972)

Hemmer, B., 'Ibsen and the Realistic Problem Drama', in J. McFarlane (ed.) *The Cambridge Companion to Ibsen* (Cambridge University Press, 1994)

Ibsen, H., 'Notes made for A Doll's House 1878', in *The Oxford Ibsen* Vol. 5 (1960)

James, H., *The Scenic Art* (Allan Wade, 1957)

Lone Marker, F. and L., 'Ibsen and the Twentieth Century Stage', in J. McFarlane (ed.) *The Cambridge Companion to Ibsen* (Cambridge University Press, 1994)

McFarlane, J. (ed.), *The Cambridge Companion to Ibsen* (Cambridge University Press, 1994)

McFarlane, J. (ed.), *Four Major Plays – Henrik Ibsen* (Oxford University Press, 1981)

McFarlane, J., 'Ibsen's Working Methods', in J. McFarlane (ed.), *The Cambridge Companion to Ibsen* (Cambridge University Press, 1994)

Meyer, M. (ed.), *A Doll's House* (Methuen Student Edition, 1985)

Meyer, M., *Ibsen: A Biography* (Doubleday, 1971)

Miller, A., *Death of a Salesman* (Penguin, 1965)

Miller, A., *Ibsen and the Drama of Today*, in J. McFarlane (ed.) *The Cambridge Companion to Ibsen* (Cambridge University Press, 1994)

Osborne, J., *Look Back in Anger* (Faber and Faber, 1957)

Pinter, H., *The Homecoming* (Faber and Faber, 1991)

Woolf, V., *A Room of One's Own* (Cambridge University Press, 1995)

Worral, N. (ed.), *A Doll's House* (Methuen, 1985)

CAMBRIDGE LITERATURE

✦